Air Fryer Recipes

Step-By-Step Guide To Healthy, Easy & Delicious Kitchen-Tested Recipes

Susmita Dutta

Global Book
Publishing

Air Fryer Recipes
Step-By-Step Guide To Healthy, Easy & Delicious Kitchen-Tested Recipes
Susmita Dutta
©2022 Susmita Dutta. All rights reserved.

ISBN: 978-1-956193-21-3
Book Design & Publishing done by:
Global Book Publishing
www.globalbookpublishing.com

Disclaimer: The Publisher and the Authors make no representations or warranties with respect to the accuracy and completeness of this work and specially disclaim all warranties, including without limitation warranties of fitness for a particular purpose. No warranty may be created or extended by sales or promotional materials. The advice and strategies contain herein may not be suitable for every situation. This work is sold with the understanding that the Publisher is not engaged in rendering legal, accounting, or other professional services. If professional assistance is required, the services of a competent professional person should be sought. Neither the Publisher nor the Author shall be liable for the damages arising here from. The fact that an organization or website is referred to in this work as a citation or potential source of further information does not mean that the Author or the Publisher endorses the information the organization or the website may provide or recommendations it may make. Further, readers should be aware that internet websites listed in this work may have changed or disappeared between when this work was written and when it is used.

This book is dedicated to my husband (Akshay) who has always encouraged me and eats all the foods made by me (Yumm Or Yuck) with a happy smile ☺

Table of Contents

Air Fryer Tips and Tricks 8

Air Fryer Accessories 9

Air Fryer Cooking Chart 10

STARTERS

1. Air Fried Bhaja (Bong style) 12
2. Air Fried Carrot 13
3. Air Fried Gnocchi 14
4. Air Fried Falafel 15
5. Banana Chips 16
6. Bagel Pizza Bites 17
7. Breaded Zucchini Fries 18
8. Calamari 19
9. Calzone 20
10. Cream Cheese Stuffed Croissant 21
11. Cream Cheese Stuffed Mushroom 22
12. Crispy Chickpeas 23
13. Crispy Spinach Balls (Palak Pakoda) 24
14. Dahi (Yogurt) Ke Kabab 25
15. Dinner Rolls 26
16. Egg Puffs 28
17. Garlic Bread Toast 30
18. Gobhi Pakoda (Cauliflower Bites) 31
19. Green Beans 32
20. Grilled Cheese Sandwich 33
21. Hotdog Wraps 34
22. Jalapeno Cheddar Pull-apart Biscuit 35
23. Jalapeno Poppers 36
24. Onion Pakoda 37
25. Paneer (Tofu)-Stuffed Bell Pepper 38
26. Potato French Fries 39
27. Potato Puff Pastry 40
28. Potato Puff Pastry Pinwheels 41
29. Quesadilla 42
30. Roasted Baby Potato 43
31. Roasted Brussels Sprouts 44

32. Roasted Corn on The Cob 45
33. Roasted Vegetable Soup 46
34. Salmon Fingers 47
35. Shrimp Cakes/Patty 48
36. Spinach Quiche 49
37. Spring Rolls 50
38. Stuffed Eggplant 51
39. Stuffed Tomatoes 52
40. Sweet Potato French Fries 53
41. Toasted Cheese Baguette 54
42. Tofu/Paneer Puffs 55
43. Tomato Carrot Soup 56

MAIN-COURSE

1. Baked Mac and Cheese 58
2. BBQ Cauliflower Poppers 59
3. BBQ Chicken Wings 60
4. Bengali Mach (Fish) Bhaja 61
5. Breaded Shrimps 62
6. Cauliflower Steak 63
7. Chicken and Mushroom with More! 64
8. Chicken Biryani 65
9. Chicken Chimichanga 66
10. Chicken Corn Taquitos 67
11. Chicken Empanadas 68
12. Chicken Fajitas 69
13. Chicken Kabab 70
14. Chicken Lasagna 71
15. Chicken Manchurian Gravy 73
16. Chicken Meat Balls Gravy 75
17. Chicken Meatloaf 76
18. Chicken Pie 77
19. Coconut Shrimp 78
20. Cream Cheese Stuffed Salmon 79
21. Fish Cutlet 80
22. Garlic Butter Roasted Salmon 81
23. Garlic Butter Shrimp 82
24. Garlic Parmesan Chicken Wings 83
25. Gobi Manchurian 84
26. Imitation Crab Cake 86
27. Lemon Pepper Chicken Thighs 87
28. Paneer/Tofu Tikka 88
29. Panko Crusted Basa/Cod 89
30. Potato Chicken Drumstick 90
31. Roasted Chicken Legs 91
33. Roasted Whole Chicken 92

34. Simple Veggie Pizza 93
35. Sorshe Hilsha (Ilish) Bhapa (Bong Style) 95
36. Stuffed Chicken Breast 96
37. Sweet Potato Chat (Oh! So Indian) 97
38. Tofu/Paneer Tacos 98
39. Tomato Garlic Feta Pasta 99

DESSERT

1. Air Fried Oreo 102
2. Baked Rasgulla 103
3. Banana-Walnut Choco Chips Muffin 104
4. Blueberry Pie 105
5. Blueberry Puffs 106
6. Chocolate Chip Cookie 107
7. Chocolate Lava Cake 108
8. Chocolate Pound Cake 109
9. Cinnamon Apple Puff 110
10. Cinnamon Donut (Biscuits) 111
11. Cinnamon Rolls 112
12. Cream Roll 113
13. Crème Brulee 114
14. Gulab Jamun 115
15. Mini Chocolate Tart 117
16. Mini Mixed-Berry Tart 118
17. Nutella Twist 119
18. Nutella-Stuffed Croissant 120
19. Oreo Cheesecake 121
20. Raspberry Jam Biscuit 122
21. Semiya Payasam 123
21. Sugar Puff (Super Easy Dessert) 124

Cooking Conversion Chart 125
Acknowledgement 126
About Susmita! 127

Air Fryer Tips and Tricks

1. Remember to always preheat your air fryer for 3 minutes at 400°F.
2. Never preheat your air fryer with parchment paper inside, it will just blow off.
3. For extra crispy results, spray oil and coat your food halfway through cooking.
4. Use oil spray that do not cause mist while spraying (nonstick aerosol cooking sprays). They can cause damage to your air fryer.
5. Line underneath the basket with an aluminum foil for easy cleanup of the grease and oil.
6. Shake the fryer basket throughout the cooking process for even cooking.
7. Use oil that has high smoke point, for example, avocado oil.
8. When cooking meat in an air fryer, be sure to check the temperature of it.
9. Do not put air fryer over a cooking top to avoid accidents.
10. Use a slice of bread under the air fryer basket to soak up grease.
11. Use air fryer (not microwave) to reheat breads and meat for crispier, tastier leftovers.
12. Do not put liquid inside the air fryer. It would cause smoke as the liquid will fly off during cooking.
13. Wipe off the grease completely from air fryer basket before washing it with water.
14. Clean your air fryer after every use.
15. Always seal a cook the salmon. This will avoid it getting dry in the frying process.
16. Magic eraser works fantastic on the inside of an air fryer.
17. Avoid overcrowding the basket.
18. For battered foods, always line your air fryer basket with parchment paper.
19. Do not grease the basket and trays. Instead, line with parchment paper or aluminum foil for easy cleaning.
20. Sprinkle some water to the air fryer drawer when cooking bacon to prevent smoking.
21. You can re-use the drippings that collect in the clean air fryer basket (like bacon fat!) to make pan sauces and gravies.
22. Shake the basket a few times during cooking to make sure everything is browning evenly.
23. For larger items (like whole chicken cutlets or pork chops), cook them in a single layer and don't stack them.
24. To avoid the burning of the breads, cakes and etc. Cover it will a sheet of aluminum foil while cooking.
25. From French fries to chicken nuggets to gnocchi, you can cook just about any frozen food in the air fryer.
26. Use foil or parchment paper to make cleanup easier.
27. Make sure there's at least 5 inches of space around your air fryer.
28. Use air fryer to toast the nuts and croutons.
29. Mix your seasonings with oil before adding/spreading them onto your foods/meat to prevent them from blowing around.
30. Use air fryer for baking of the savory items. "Baking" in an air fryer is not only possible but super easy.
31. And you can "hard-boil" eggs in an air fryer, too.

Air Fryer Accessories

	If you want to grill, sear, roast or fry in a larger air fryer you'll want to add this grill pan to your accessories list. The perforated holes in the bottom allow air to circulate, which the company says helps to distribute heat evenly and allow grease and oils to drip away from your food.
	Items coming out of the air fryer can be very hot to the touch, so make sure you have a set of tongs on-hand to pull out loose foods like chicken nuggets or other accessories including a cake pan or silicone mold.
	You don't need oil to cook your food in an air fryer, but a little spritz can make your food crispier. You can also give your air fryer basket, cake pan or any other accessories a quick spritz before cooking to prevent food from sticking.
	If you're worried about your food sticking to the bottom of your air fryer or baking pan, make sure to keep these parchment paper liners handy. They'll reduce the amount of food residue on your fryer, making cleanup just a little easier.
	This reversible air fryer rack is dual-purpose accessory. It can function as a rack for your air fryer, allowing air to circulate around your food and ensure it is evenly cooked and crispy, and it can double as a cooling rack.
	Racks add versatility to the air fryer. Sold in a two-pack, the racks maximize surface cooking. Additionally, use the skewer rack for kabobs or other dishes like peach-bourbon wings. Bonus: These racks are dishwasher-safe for easy cleanup.
	Use a barrel pan or round pan for breads, pizza, cakes and more.
	For meat loafs and banana breads and cakes, these silicone loaf pans will come in handy. They're the perfect size for nestling in your air fryer, but you can use them in the microwave and oven, too.
	Correct cooking times are the key to air-frying, but a double-check is never a bad idea. An instant-read thermometer can make sure your food is cooked through in even the thickest spots. If you're unsure what the temperature should be, check out this guide to food-safe cooking temperatures.
	This silicone muffin tray makes air-frying your favorite comfort foods a breeze. Plus, it's dishwasher-safe for easy cleanup.
	If kababs are on your favorite food items list then these use and throw wooden skewers should be on your "must try" list, this skewer makes cooking a breeze. You can also use steel skewers if you prefer to have them for a long term basis.

FOOD	TEMPERATURE	AIR-FRYER TIME
Meat and Seafood		
Bacon	400°F	5-10 minutes
Bone-In Pork Chops	400°F	4-5 minutes per side
Brats	400°F	8-10 minutes
Burgers	350°F	8-10 minutes
Chicken Breast	375°F	22-23 minutes
Chicken Tenders	400°F	14-16 minutes
Chicken Thighs	400°F	25 minutes
Chicken Wings	375°F	10-12 minutes
Cod	370°F	8-10 minutes
Meatballs	400°F	7-10 minutes
Meat Loaf	325°F	35-45 minutes
Pork Chops	375°F	12-15 minutes
Salmon	400°F	5-7 minutes
Sausage Patties	400°F	8-10 minutes
Shrimp	375°F	8 minutes
Steak	400°F	7-14 minutes
Tilapia	400°F	6-8 minutes
Vegetables		
Asparagus	375°F	4-6 minutes
Baked Potatoes	400°F	35-45 minutes
Broccoli	400°F	8-10 minutes
Brussels Sprouts	350°F	15-18 minutes
Butternut Squash (cubed)	375°F	20-25 minutes
Carrots	375°F	15-25 minutes
Cauliflower	400°F	10-12 minutes
Green Beans	375°F	16-20 minutes
Peppers	375°F	8-10 minutes
Sweet Potatoes (cubed)	375°F	15-20 minutes
Zucchini	400°F	12 minutes
Fried Foods		
Fries	400°F	10-20 minutes
Pickles	400°F	14-20 minutes
Potato Chips	360°F	15-17 minutes
Frozen Foods		
Corn Dogs	400°F	8 minutes
Mozzarella Sticks	400°F	6-8 minutes
Tater Tots	400°F	12-15 minutes
Bakes and Breads		
Brownies	325°F	40-45 minutes
Cookies	325°F	8-10 minutes
Cupcakes	325°F	11-13 minutes
Garlic Bread	350°F	2-3 minutes
Mains/Snacks		
Mini Pizzas	400°F	4-5 minutes
Quesadillas	375°F	5-7 minutes

STARTER

Air Fried Bhaja (Bong Style)

Prep 15 Min	Cook 15 Min	Four Servings

INGREDIENTS

- 3-5 Teaspoons of Turmeric Powder
- 1-2 Teaspoons of Salt
- 1 Large Eggplant (Sliced into 4-5 cm Half Circles)
- 1 Large Potato (Sliced into 1 cm Circles)
- 1 Large Bitter Gourd (Sliced into 1-2 cm Circles)
- 2 Tablespoons Cooking Oil

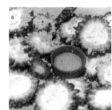
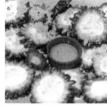

DIRECTIONS

Step 1: Preheat your air fryer for 3 minutes at 350°F.

Step 2: Slice your Vegetable into thin slices about 1 cm for Potatoes, 1-2 cm for Bitter Gourd and 4-5 cm for Eggplant.

Step 3: Place Eggplant, potatoes, bitter gourd on a plate (separately of course). Rub the turmeric powder and salt mixture on to the vegetable pieces.

Step 4 : Once the air fryer is preheated add a few slices of the veggies (eggplant/potatoes/bitter gourd) on the wire rack of the basket. Spray/brush vegetable/canola oil on top of the veggies.

Step 5: Air fry at 350°F for 15 minutes. Flip it halfway, continue to cook till you see them golden brown and crisp. Follow the same with rest of the slices.

Note: Always fry the vegetables separately. You can also fry pumpkin, carrots, and other veggies this way.

Air Fried Carrot

Prep 5 Min	Cook 12 Min	Four Servings

INGREDIENTS

- 1 Teaspoon of Chili Flakes
- 1 Tablespoon Butter/Oil
- ½ Teaspoon of Crushed Black Pepper Corns
- ½ Tablespoon of Dried Parsley
- 1lb Carrots

DIRECTIONS

Step 1: You'll need one 1 lb bag of baby carrots. Rinse and pat dry the carrots. Patting them dry will keep them from steaming while being cooked and help create a roasted, fried texture.

Step 2: Mix the baby carrots, butter, chili flakes, and dried parsley together, make sure carrots are well-coated.

Step 3: Set the air fryer at 350°F and add in the carrot mix.

Step 4: Cook for 8-10 minutes. After 12 minutes stir the carrots around, cook for 5 more minutes.

Air Fried Gnocchi

Prep 10 Min	Cook 10 Min	Four Servings

INGREDIENTS

- 2 Cups Store Bought Gnocchi
- 1 Tablespoon Melted Butter
- 1 Teaspoon Onion Powder
- 1 Teaspoon Dried Parsley
- 1 Teaspoon Garlic Salt
- 1 Tablespoon Grated Parmesan
- Chili Flakes to Taste

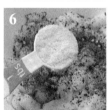

DIRECTIONS

Step 1: Boil the Gnocchi for 5 to 7 minutes or until it starts floating. Strain it and keep aside.

Step 2: In a bowl, toss together the boiled gnocchi, butter, garlic salt, onion powder, dried parsley, grated parmesan, and chili flakes.

Step 3: Transfer the seasoned gnocchi to the air fryer basket.

Step 4: Air fry for 8 to 10 minutes at 375°F for crispy crunchy gnocchi. Be sure to shake the basket at the halfway mark.

Air Fried Falafel

Prep 10 Min	Cook 18 Min	Four Servings

INGREDIENTS

- 5 Cloves of Garlic
- 1 Cup Canned/Hard Boiled Fresh Parsley
- 1 Cup Chickpea
- 1 Tablespoon Baking Powder
- ½ Tablespoon Paprika Powder
- 1 Teaspoon Salt
- ½ Tablespoon Cumin Powder
- 1 Fresh Green Chili
- Oil Spray

DIRECTIONS

Step 1: In a blender, place the ingredients chickpea, garlic, parsley and green chili. Blend them till it looks a little crushed, and now place all the spices and blend again till it looks like a thick paste.

Step 2: Make even sized balls from the falafel mixture.

Step 3: Place at least 10 pieces in the air fryer, don't over crowd it.

Step 4: Spray/Brush oil generously. Air fry at 375°F for 10 minutes. Take out, give it a good shake and fry again for 8 minutes.

Banana Chips

Prep 10 Min	Cook 10 Min	Four Servings

INGREDIENTS

- ½ Teaspoon Turmeric Powder
- 1 Teaspoon Salt
- 1 Tablespoon Coconut Oil
- 1-2 Large Plantain

DIRECTIONS

Step 1: Peel the banana with the help of a peeler.

Step 2: Slice the bananas into thin slices, about ¼ inch thick (can use chips slicer).

Step 3: Put the banana slices into the bowl toss in the turmeric powder, salt, and coconut oil. Coat the chips with the spice mix.

Step 4: Place the banana slices in a single layer in the air fryer at 375°F for 7-9 minutes. Work in batches if needed since overcrowding will result in soggy banana chips.

Step 5: Flipping over halfway through cooking time. Remove from air fryer and let it cool before enjoying for the crispiest air fryer banana chips.

Bagel Pizza Bites

Prep 5 Min	Cook 5 Min	Six Servings

INGREDIENTS

- 3 Bagel (Sliced into Half)
- ½ Cup Pizza Sauce
- Fresh Mozzarella Cheese
- 2 Tablespoons Chopped Onion
- 2 Tablespoons Chopped Yellow Pepper
- 2 Tablespoons Chopped Red Pepper
- Dried Oregano and Chili Flakes

DIRECTIONS

Step 1: Sliced the bagel into half.

Step 2: Spread generous amount of pizza sauce onto the bagel. Top it with fresh mozzarella and onion-pepper mix. (See Image 3)

Step 3: Sprinkle some oregano and chili flakes.

Step 4: Air fry at 375°F for 5 minutes.

Breaded Zucchini Fries

Prep 10 Min	Cook 15 Min	Four Servings

INGREDIENTS

- 1 Egg
- 1 Cup Breadcrumbs
- ½ Cup Parmesan Cheese
- 2 Medium Size Zucchini
- ½ Cup All-Purpose Flour

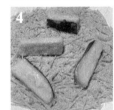

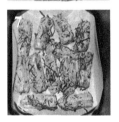

DIRECTIONS

Step 1: Slice the zucchini into long and thick pieces.

Step 2: First, toss it in the flour, then nicely coated with beaten egg, and lastly coat it with the mixture of breadcrumbs with parmesan cheese.

Step 3: Place at least 10-15 zucchini fries into the preheat air fryer.

Step 4: Generously spray with cooking oil.

Step 5: Air fry for at least 7-9 minutes at 360°F on both sides.

Note: You can also follow the same recipe for round zucchini slices.

Calamari

Prep 15 Min	Cook 15 Min	Four Servings

INGREDIENTS

- 1 Cup All-Purpose Flour
- 1 Large Egg
- 2 Cups Panko Breadcrumbs
- 1 Teaspoon Himalayan Pink Salt
- ½ Teaspoon Paprika
- ¼ Teaspoon Ground Black Pepper
- 1 Pound Calamari Rings, Cut into Circles and Patted Dry
- Nonstick Cooking Spray

DIRECTIONS

Step 1: Preheat an air fryer to 400°F for 3 minutes.

Step 2: Combine flour, salt, black pepper, and paprika in a plate, whisk egg in a separate bowl. Take panko breadcrumbs in the third plate.

Step 3: Coat calamari rings first in flour, then in egg mixture, and finally in Panko breadcrumbs mixture.

Step 4: Place rings in the basket of the air fryer so that none are overlapping. Work in batches if needed. Spray the calamari rings with nonstick cooking spray.

Step 5: Air fry at 360°F for 10 minutes. Flip rings, spray with nonstick cooking spray and cook for another 3-5 minutes.

Step 6: Serve while hot and with a tartar sauce or your preferred dipping.

Calzone

Prep 10 Min	Cook 20 Min	Four Servings

INGREDIENTS

- ½ Cup Butter
- 1 Teaspoon Sugar
- 1 Teaspoon Garlic Salt
- 1 Teaspoon Paprika Powder
- Homemade Dough (See Pizza from Scratch Section)
- Sliced Bell Pepper
- Sliced Onion
- Alfredo Pizza Sauce
- Shredded Mozzarella Cheese

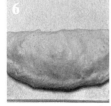

DIRECTIONS

Step 1: First, in a small bowl, take of butter, paprika powder, and garlic salt. Give them a nice mix and set aside.

Step 2: Now get your homemade dough. Roll the dough into an 8 inches circle, just like in the given image.

Step 3: Spread pizza sauce on the rolled dough.

Step 4: Then put some bell pepper, onion, and top it with shredded cheese before sealing the edges of the dough. Brush the butter mixture on top.

Step 5: Air fry at 375°F for 20-25 minutes.

Note: Feel free to use any spreading sauce if your choice (Marinara, Alfredo, or Schezwan).

Cream Cheese Stuffed Croissant

Prep 5 Min	Cook 15 Min	Two Servings

INGREDIENTS

- Croissant Dough/Sheet (Store Bought)
- ½ Cup Cream Cheese
- ½ Cup Shredded Cheddar Cheese
- 2-3 Tablespoons Jalapeno (Chopped)
- 1 Teaspoon Garlic Powder
- 1 Tablespoon Dried Parsley

DIRECTIONS

Step 1: For cream cheese filing, combine together the cream cheese, jalapeno, shredded cheddar, dried parsley, and garlic powder.

Step 2: Unroll the dough sheet and cut out the triangles for easy rolling.

Step 3: Spread generous amount of the cream cheese filling onto the croissant sheets. (See Image 4)

Step 4: For rolling you have to start from the widest end to the smallest point. (See Image 5)

Step 5: Following the same way, roll up all the croissant.

Step 6: Air fry at 360°F for 10 minutes. Flip and air fry again for 5 minutes on the other side.

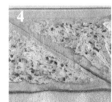
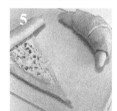
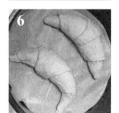

Cream Cheese Stuffed Mushroom

Prep 10 Min	Cook 10 Min	Four Servings

INGREDIENTS

- 8-10 Medium Size Mushroom
- ¼ Cup Fresh Parsley (Chopped)
- 1 Tablespoon Italian Seasoning
- 1 Cup Cream Cheese
- ¼ Cup Parmesan Cheese
- ¼ Cup Mushroom Stalks (Chopped)
- 1 Teaspoon Chili Flakes
- ½ Cup Panko Breadcrumbs
- Salt to Taste

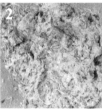

DIRECTIONS

Step 1: Using a damp cloth, gently clean the mushrooms. Remove stems and chop to use.

Step 2: Combine cream cheese, Parmesan cheese, mushroom stalks, Italian seasoning, parsley, chili flakes and salt in a bowl.

Step 3: Stuff the filling into the mushrooms, press it in to fill the cavity with the back of a small spoon, and roll it onto the breadcrumbs. (See Images 3 and 4)

Step 4: Spray the air fryer basket with cooking spray and set mushrooms inside. Depending on the size of your air fryer, you may have to do 2 batches.

Step 5: Air fry at 350°F for 10 minutes (or until browned/crispy). Repeat with remaining mushrooms.

Crispy Chickpeas

Prep 5 Min	Cook 15 Min	Four Servings

INGREDIENTS

- 1 Can of Chickpeas
- ½ Tablespoon Paprika Powder
- 1 Teaspoon Onion Powder
- 1 Tablespoon of Avocado Oil
- 1 Teaspoon Salt

DIRECTIONS

Step 1: Drain the water from the chickpeas and pat them dry.

Step 2: In a large bowl, place the chickpeas and add in the paprika, avocado oil, salt, and onion powder. Give it a good mix.

Step 3: Place all of the chickpeas into the preheated air fryer (avoid overlapping).

Step 4: Air fry at 375°F for 12 minutes. Take it out, give it a good shake and air fry again for 5-7 minutes or until golden brown and it has a crunchy texture.

Note: Allow the air fried chickpeas to completely cool down before storing them in an air-tight container.

Crispy Spinach Balls (Palak Pakoda)

Prep 10 Min	Cook 10 Min	Four Servings

INGREDIENTS

- 3 Cups Raw Spinach (Chopped)
- ¼ Cup Sliced Onions
- 2-3 Pieces of Green Chili (Chopped)
- ½ Teaspoon Carom Seeds
- ½ Teaspoon Salt
- ¼ Cup Bengal Gram Flour (Besan)
- Oil Spray

DIRECTIONS

Step 1: First, chop the fresh spinach, onion, and green chili and place them in a clean bowl.

Step 2: Season with carom seeds, salt, and mix everything together.

Step 3: Now add the gram flour and mix it thoroughly.

Step 4: Shape them into balls and place them in a preheated air fryer.

Step 5: Don't overcrowd them. Place at least 8-9 pieces of it the air fryer for even cooking.

Step 6: Spray oil generously and air fry at 360°F for 7 minutes. Take out and flip them and cook again for 3-5 minutes (adjust cooking time based on crispiness).

Dahi (Yogurt) Ke Kabab

Prep 15 Min	Cook 15 Min	Four Servings

INGREDIENTS

- 1 Cup Hung Curd
- 1 Teaspoon Chili Flakes
- 1 Tablespoon Fresh Minced Coriander
- ¼ Cup Roasted Gram Flour
- 2 Tablespoons Minced Onion
- 1 Teaspoon Salt
- 1 Cup Breadcrumbs
- Oil Spray

DIRECTIONS

Step 1: Dry roast the gram flour in a hot pan for 4-5 minutes (except breadcrumbs).

Step 2: In a clean bowl, toss all the ingredients and give it a good mix. (See Image 2)

Step 3: Now apply oil in your palm and take a tablespoon full of the yogurt mixture.

Step 4: Shape them into a ball and then press them slightly to form kabab shape. Coat them well with breadcrumbs.

Step 5: Spray oil generously, air fry at 375°F for 7 minutes. Flip them and air fry again for 3-5 minutes.

Note: For best result, hang the curd/yogurt overnight in a refrigerator.

Dinner Rolls

Prep 120 Min	Cook 15 Min	Four Servings

INGREDIENTS

- 1 Tablespoon Active Dry Yeast (1 Sachet)
- ½ Cup Warm Milk
- 2 ¼ Cups All-Purpose Flour
- 1 Tablespoon Granulated Sugar
- ½ Teaspoon Salt
- 2 Tablespoons Olive Oil

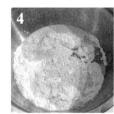 
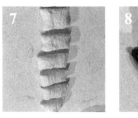 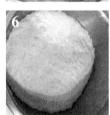
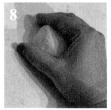

DIRECTIONS

Step 1: To the warm milk, add sugar and yeast. Give it a good mix. Keep aside for 3-5 minutes or until frothy on top. (See Image 3)

Step 2: In a mixing bowl, add the flour and salt. Give it a good mix.

Step 3: Now add the activated yeast mixture and oil. Mix everything to form a soft dough.

Step 4: Keep kneading it for 5 to 6 minutes (until the gluten forms/looks smooth).

Step 5: Rest the dough in a warm place to rise for 1 to 1.5 hours.

Step 6: Once the dough has doubled in size, punch it down releasing some of the air. Knead again for a minute or two.

Step 7: Divide the dough into 6 equal pieces and roll into balls.

To Be Continued ...

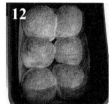

Step 8: Allow the dinner rolls to rest and rise for 15 minutes.

Step 9: In a small bowl, stir or whisk an egg and then brush the tops of the rolls with an egg wash.

Step 10: Preheat the air fryer for 3 minutes at 400°F. Air Fry at 400°F for 12 minutes until the tops of the rolls are golden brown. Check the bottom of the rolls for doneness as well. If they are not completely set on the bottom, you can add a couple of minutes.

Pro Tip: Place a sheet of foil paper on top of the dinner rolls to avoid burning.

Egg Puff

Prep 10 Min	Cook 15 Min	Six Servings

INGREDIENTS

- 2 Tablespoons Minced Garlic
- 1 Cup Chopped Large Red Onion
- 1 Cup Chopped Tomatoes
- ½ Tablespoon Red Chili Powder
- 1 Teaspoon Cumin Powder
- 1 Teaspoon Coriander Powder
- ¼ Teaspoon Turmeric Powder
- Pastry Sheets
- 2-3 Hard-boiled Eggs
- Salt to Taste
- 1 Tablespoon Olive Oil

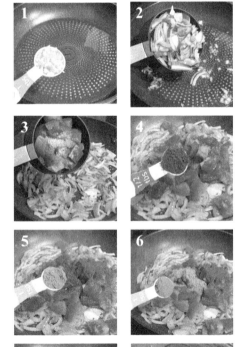

DIRECTIONS

Making of the Filling:

Step 1: Heat oil in a pan, add in the garlic and saute it till golden brown.

Step 2: Add the onion and fry for a minute.

Step 3: Now add tomatoes and all the dry spices. Give it a good mix, cook for about a minute, and then put the lid and let it simmer for 5 minutes.

Step 4: Open the lid and cook for 2 to 3 minutes, or until all the water evaporates.

Step 5: Let the filling cool down for a few minutes while we prepare the pastry sheets.

To Be Continued ...

Making of Puffs

Step 6: Cut the hard-boiled egg into two.

Step 7: Cut the pastry sheets into 6 inches square of equal sizes.

Step 8: Put 2 tablespoons of the filling into the center of the pastry sheets and put the half egg on top of the filling. (See Image 11)

Step 9: Fold the sides of the pastry sheet together, just like in the given images.

Step 10: Place at least 3-4 pieces of the egg puffs into the preheated air fryer.

Step 11: Air fry at 375°F for 7 minutes.

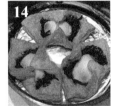

29

Garlic Bread Toast

Prep 10 Min	Cook 7 Min	Four Servings

INGREDIENTS

- 1 Tablespoon Dried Parsley
- 3-5 Big Garlic Cloves Minced
- 6 Small Cubes of Butter (3 Tablespoons)
- Salt to Taste
- Baguette — Sliced to Your Choice of Thickness

DIRECTIONS

Step 1: Mix together the softened butter, minced garlic, salt, and dried parsley.

Step 2: Spread the mixture onto sliced baguettes or bread of your choice. (Spread on both sides.)

Step 3: Place the garlic bread into the air fryer basket in a single layer.

Step 4: Air fry at 375°F for 5-7 minutes.

Gobhi Pakoda (Cauliflower Bites)

Prep 20 Min	Cook 20 Min	Four Servings

INGREDIENTS

- 15-20 Raw Cauliflower Florets
- ¼ Cup Bengal Gram Flour (Besan)
- 1 Tablespoon Corn Starch
- ½ Tablespoon Paprika
- 1 Teaspoon Garlic Salt
- Oil Spray

DIRECTIONS

Step 1: In a large bowl, combine all the dry ingredients and give it a good mix.

Step 2: Gradually add water and make a thick consistency batter.

Step 3: Coat the cauliflower florets evenly with the flour mixture.

Step 4: Place the coated cauliflower florets in an air fryer basket. Spray oil generously.

Step 5: Air fry at 350°F for 12-15 minutes. Flip it half-way through and air fry again.

Note: Line the air fryer basket with parchment paper. This will avoid sticking of the pakodas to the basket.

Green Beans

Prep 5 Min	Cook 10 Min	Two Servings

INGREDIENTS

- 1 Pound Green Beans
- 1 Tablespoon Minced Garlic
- ¼ Teaspoon Ground Pepper
- 1 Tablespoon Olive/Avocado Oil
- 2 Tablespoons Grated Parmesan

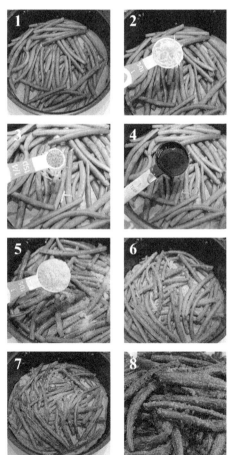

DIRECTIONS

Step 1: First, wash and pat dry the green beans. Place them all in the air fryer basket directly.

Step 2: Toss in the ingredients (minced garlic, pepper powder, olive oil, and the grated parmesan). Give them a good mix and they are ready to go.

Step 3: Air fry them at 375°F for 5 minutes. Take them out, give a good shake and air fry again for 5 minutes.

Grilled Cheese Sandwich

Prep 5 Min	Cook 5 Min	Two Servings

INGREDIENTS

- 2 Bread Slices
- 2 Tablespoons Butter
- Cheddar Cheese
- Provolone/Mozzarella Cheese

DIRECTIONS

Step 1: Start by buttering the bread slices.

Step 2: On one piece of bread, add the cheddar cheese plus the mozzarella or provolone cheese.

Step 3: Air fry at 400°F for 5 minutes or until the top is crispy brown.

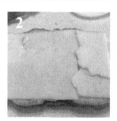

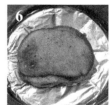

Hotdog Wraps

Prep 5 Min	Cook 12 Min	Four Servings

INGREDIENTS

- Wiener Wraps (Store Bought)
- 1 Tablespoon Butter
- ½ Teaspoon Garlic Salt
- 1 Teaspoon Dried Oregano
- ½ Teaspoon Chili Flakes
- 4 Pieces of Regular Size Hotdog
- 4 Pieces Mozzarella Cheese Sticks

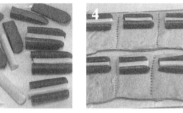

DIRECTIONS

Step 1: In a bowl, combine butter, chili flakes, garlic salt and oregano. Give it a mix and set aside.

Step 2: Slice the hotdog into half and then slit from the middle, just like in the images.

Step 3: Slice the cheese stick into half as well.

Step 4: Now sandwich the cheese between hotdogs slices (hotdog-cheese-hotdog), just like the image 3.

Step 5: Cut the weiner wraps into equal sizes and place the hotdog-cheese sandwich on one corner.

Step 6: Now roll it and seal the wraps.

Step 7: Place the weiner wraps in an air fryer basket and brush the spiced butter mixture on top.

Step 8: Air fry at 360°F for 8 minutes. Flip and air fry again for 5 minutes.

Step 9: Serve them with ketchup or any dipping sauce you prefer.

Note: Instead of weiner wraps, you can also use croissants rolls dough as well.

34

Jalapeno Cheddar Pull-apart Biscuit

Prep 10 Min	Cook 20 Min	Four Servings

INGREDIENTS

- Flaky Biscuit Dough (You Can Use Pizza Dough as Well)
- 1 Tablespoon Minced Garlic
- 1 Tablespoon Minced Jalapeno
- 2 Tablespoons Melted Butter
- ½ Cup Shredded Cheddar Cheese
- 1 Tablespoon Dried Parsley

DIRECTIONS

Step 1: Using a sharp knife cut each biscuit piece into little pieces. (See Image 1)

Step 2: In a large mixing bowl, add the biscuit pieces, minced garlic, jalapeno, melted butter, grated cheese, and dried parsley together.

Step 3: Add the biscuit dough to the greased Bundt Pan. Cover the pan with foil paper and poke some holes in it to release the air.

Step 4: Air fry at 375°F for 17-20 minutes.

Note: You can also make muffins as well for easy sharing.

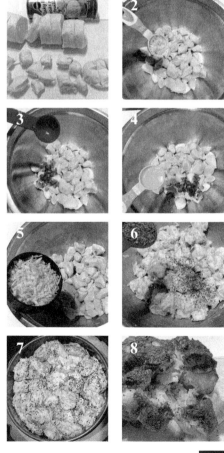

Jalapeno Poppers

Prep 10 Min	Cook 10 Min	Four Servings

INGREDIENTS

- 1 Cup Cream Cheese
- ½ Cup Shredded Cheddar Cheese
- ¼ Cup Panko Breadcrumbs
- 1 Tablespoon Dried Parsley
- ¼ Teaspoon Garlic Powder
- 3-5 Jalapeno Peppers
- Oil Spray

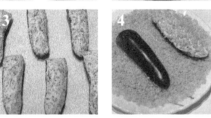

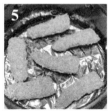
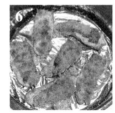

DIRECTIONS

Step 1: In a bowl, combine cream cheese, shredded cheddar, dried parsley, garlic powder. Give it a good mix and your filling is ready.

Step 2: Cut the jalapeno into half and remove the seeds.

Step 3: Fill each jalapeno with the cream cheese filling mixture and top with breadcrumbs. (See Images 3 and 4)

Step 4: Spray oil and air fry at 375°F for 7-9 minutes Or until the panko breadcrumbs is golden brown and crispy.

Onion Pakoda

Prep 10 Min	Cook 10 Min	Four Servings

INGREDIENTS

- 1 Teaspoon Coriander Powder
- ¼ Cup Bengal Gram Flour (Besan)
- 2 Cups Thinly Sliced Onions (2 Medium Size)
- 2-3 Pieces Green Chili (Chopped)
- ¼ Teaspoon Salt
- Oil Spray

DIRECTIONS

Step 1: In a bowl, mix together chopped onion, green chilies, coriander powder, and salt.

Step 2: After that add the gram flour and mix everything very well (use hand if possible).

Step 3: Make equal sized ball-like portion and place it in the preheated air fryer.

Step 4: Spray oil generously and air fry at 350°F for 8 minutes. Take out, flip and air fry for 4 minutes on the other side.

Step 5: Serve hot with tomato ketchup.

Note: I use the same pakoda's for making Indian kadhi, sabji etc.

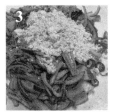

Paneer (Tofu)-Stuffed Bell Pepper

Prep 15 Min	Cook 20 Min	Four Servings

INGREDIENTS

- 2 Bell Peppers
- 1 Cup Shredded Paneer/Tofu
- ¼ Cup Green Peas
- ¼ Cup Frozen/Raw Potato (Finely Chopped/ Minced)
- ¼ Cup Sweetcorn
- ¼ Cup Onion (Chopped)
- ½ Tablespoon Chili Flakes
- 1 Tablespoon Schezwan Chutney (Optional)
- Salt to Taste
- Olive/Avocado Oil Spray
- ½ Cup Shredded Cheddar Cheese

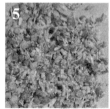
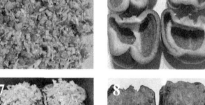

DIRECTIONS

Step 1: In a clean bowl, place all the ingredients (paneer/tofu, green peas, sweetcorn, potato, and onion). Mix everything together.

Step 2: Now add in chili flakes, salt, schezwan chutney and mix everything together.

Step 3: Slice the bell pepper in half and make sure to remove the seeds.

Step 4: Take the filling mixture you just made and stuff them inside the bell peppers. Make sure it's full.

Step 5: Place them into the preheated air fryer and spray with olive/avocado oil spray.

Step 6: Air fry at 350°F for 15 minutes.

Step 7: Take them out and top it with shredded cheddar cheese and air fry them again at 350°F for 5 more minutes.

Potato French Fries

Prep 5 Min	Cook 10 Min	Two Servings

INGREDIENTS

- 2 Large Potatoes
- Cooking Oil Spray
- 1 Teaspoon Salt
- 1 Teaspoon Ground Pepper

DIRECTIONS

Step 1: Preheat an air fryer to 400°F for 3 minutes and spray the basket with nonstick spray.

Step 2: Cut the potato in half lengthwise, then into ¼-inch slices. Cut the slices into ¼-inch sticks. (See Image 1)

Step 3: Put the fries in a bowl and soak them in ice-cold water for 5 minutes.

Step 4: Drain the water and pat dry with kitchen towel.

Step 5: Toss the fries with the oil in a medium bowl, then sprinkle with salt and ground pepper. Working in batches, if necessary.

Step 6: Air fry at 360°F for 7 minutes. Take them out, give a good shake and air fry again for 3-5 minutes.

Potato Puff Pastry

Prep 20 Min	Cook 20 Min	Four Servings

INGREDIENTS

- ½ Teaspoon Cumin Seed
- Fresh Curry Leaves
- ½ Cup Minced Onion
- 1 ½ Cup Mashed Potato
- ¼ Teaspoon Turmeric Powder
- ½ Tablespoon Coriander Powder
- 1 Teaspoon Dried Fenugreek Leaves
- ½ Tablespoon Paprika Powder
- ½ Teaspoon Salt
- Coriander Leaves
- Pastry Sheets (4 inch Squares)

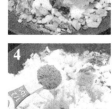

DIRECTIONS

Step 1: Heat oil in a pan, toss the cumin seed and 4-5 curry leaves. Fry them until golden brown.

Step 2: Add the onion and sauté them for a minute.

Step 3: Add mashed potato, turmeric powder, coriander powder, fenugreek leaves, paprika powder, and salt.

Step 4: Mix all the ingredients and cook for 3-5 minutes. Add the coriander leaves once done.

Step 5: Cut the pastry sheets into equal square shapes, place at least 2 tablespoons of the potato filling in the middle. (See Image 8)

Step 6: Fold and seal carefully the edges of the pastry sheet, you can use a fork to press and seal.

Step 7: Place at least 2-3 pieces of the potato puffs in an air fryer basket.

Step 8: Air fry at 350°F for 10 minutes. Flip and air fry again for 5 minutes.

Potato Puff Pastry Pinwheels

Prep 10 Min	Cook 15 Min	Four Servings

INGREDIENTS

- 1-2 Cups Mashed Potato
- ¼ Cup Minced Red Onion
- ½ Teaspoon Chili Flakes
- ½ Teaspoon Coriander Powder
- Salt to Taste
- Pastry Sheets

DIRECTIONS

Step 1: In a clean bowl, mix all the spices, mashed potato, and onion.

Step 2: Place the pastry sheets, spread the potato that you just made onto the pastry sheets. After that roll them just like the given image.

Step 3: Cut into pieces for about 4-5 cm thick.

Step 4: Flatten them into a pinwheel.

Step 5: Place them into the air fryer basket as a single layer.

Step 6: Air fry them for about 12-15 minutes or until golden brown and crispy.

Quesadilla

Prep 5 Min	Cook 5 Min	Four Servings

INGREDIENTS

- 4 Medium Flour Tortillas
- 1 Cup Shredded Cheddar Cheese Mix
- 1 Medium Red Onion, Sliced
- 2 Medium Tomatoes, Sliced
- Chili Flakes (Optional)
- Oil Spray

DIRECTIONS

Step 1: Take flour tortilla and place it on a counter top.

Step 2: Spread ¼ cup of the cheese mix on it. (See Image 1)

Step 3: Top it with Sliced tomatoes and Onions. Sprinkle some chili flakes. (Optional)

Step 4: Fold the tortilla into half (see image 4) and place it in an air fryer basket.

Step 5: Spray/brush oil on the surface and put a air fryer grilling rack on top of the tortilla (this will avoid the tortilla from opening while frying).

Step 6: Air fry at 375°F for 5 minutes.

Note: If you do not have the air fryer grilling rack then use toothpick to seal the edges of the tortilla so that they do not open up while frying.

Roasted Baby Potato

Prep 10 Min	Cook 20 Min	Four Servings

INGREDIENTS

- 1 Pound Baby Potatoes
- 1 Tablespoon Olive Oil
- 1 Teaspoon Garlic Salt
- 1 Teaspoon Onion Powder
- ½ Tablespoon Paprikar
- ½ Teaspoon Oregano
- 1 Tablespoon Grated Parmesan
- 1 Teaspoon Lemon Juice (Optional)
- Sliced Red Onion (Optional)
- Oil Spray

DIRECTIONS

Step 1: Cut the baby potatoes into halves, wash and pat dry.

Step 2: In a large bowl, toss in the baby potatoes with oil, garlic salt, onion powder, paprika, oregano, and grated parmesan. Give it a good mix.

Step 3: Place potatoes in the air fryer basket and air fry at 350°F for 10 minutes.

Step 4: Take out, give it a good shake, spray oil and air fry again at 350°F for 8 minutes.

Step 5: Add in the juice of half lemon and sliced onion before serving.

Roasted Brussels Sprouts

Prep 10 Min	Cook 10 Min	Two Servings

INGREDIENTS

- 1 Pound Brussels Sprouts
- ½ Teaspoon Garlic Salt
- 2 Teaspoons Olive Oil
- 1 Teaspoon Dried Oregano
- 1 Teaspoon Chili Flakes (Optional)

DIRECTIONS

Step 1: Trim and cut the brussels sprouts into halves. (See Image 1)

Step 2: In a bowl place the brussels sprouts and cover with a plastic wrap and microwave for 5 minutes.

Step 3: Add the spices and olive oil to the brussels sprouts and give it a good mix.

Step 4: Air fry at 350°F for 8 minutes. Take out, give it a good shake and air fry again for 5 more minutes.

Note: To make the brussels sprouts extra crispy, spray oil after first round of frying.

Roasted Corn on The Cob

Prep 5 Min	Cook 15 Min	Four Servings

INGREDIENTS

- 2 Large Sweet Corns
- 2 Tablespoons Butter
- 1 Teaspoon Paprika
- 1 Teaspoon Garlic Salt
- 1 Lemon

DIRECTIONS

Step 1: Clean and pat dry the corns.

Step 2: Mix the butter, garlic salt, and paprika powder together.

Step 3: Coat the corns with generous amount of spiced butter mixture.

Step 4: Put the corns into the preheated air fryer and air fry at 375°F for 15 minutes. Don't forget to flip it at 8 minutes.

Step 5: Serve while hot!

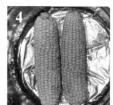

Roasted Vegetable Soup

Prep 20 Min	Cook 20 Min	Four Servings

INGREDIENTS

- Maggi Bouillon Cubes
- ½ Teaspoon Salt
- ½ Teaspoon Ground Pepper
- 2 Tablespoons Avocado/Olive Oil
- 2 Cups Cherry Tomatoes
- 1 Large Carrot
- 10-12 Cauliflower Florets
- 1 Sliced Red Bell Pepper
- 1 Medium Sliced Onion
- 8-10 Garlic Cloves
- 2 Cups Almond Milk

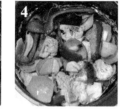

DIRECTIONS

Step 1: Line the air fryer basket with an aluminium foil and place a parchment paper on top of it (just like in the given image).

Step 2: Place the tomatoes first, then the rest of the vegetables. Mix everything together.

Step 3: Sprinkle ground pepper and salt, and drizzle oil on top.

Step 4: Air fry at 350°F for 10 minutes. Take out, give it a good shake and air fry again for 5-7 minutes.

Step 5: Now transfer the roasted veggies into the blender and add 2 cups of almond milk, 1 maggie bouillon cube and blend everything into a thick soup like consistency.

Step 6: Transfer into a soup bowl and garnish with croutons, grated parmesan and some basil.

Note: *Serve it piping hot … Best soup for winter nights!*

Salmon Fingers

Prep 10 Min	Cook 15 Min	Four Servings

INGREDIENTS

- 15-20 Salmon Finger Stripes
- 1 Tablespoon Soya Sauce
- 1 Teaspoon Paprika
- 1 Teaspoon Salt
- 1 ½ Cups Breadcrumbs
- Bowl of Water
- Oil Spray

DIRECTIONS

Step 1: Marinate the raw fish fingers with soya sauce and let it sit for at least 15 minutes.

Step 2: Season the breadcrumbs with salt and paprika.

Step 3: Coat the marinated fish strips with spiced breadcrumbs.

Step 4: Now dip the coated fish fingers in a bowl of water and quickly remove them.

Step 5: Coat the wet fish fingers again with the spiced breadcrumbs.

Step 6: Once the fish sticks are thoroughly coated, place them in the Air Fryer basket, make sure that they're not overlapping.

Step 7: Spray oil generously to coat the fish fingers. Air fry at 375°F for 12 minutes, flip, and cook for 3 more minutes.

Step 8: Serve with tartar sauce.

Note: To make raw fish fingers, slice the salmon fillet into 2 inches thick strips. You can use any other fish of your choice too.

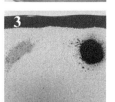

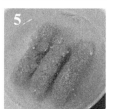

Shrimp Cakes/Patty

Prep 10 Min	Cook 15 Min	Four Servings

INGREDIENTS

- 1 Teaspoon Onion Powder
- ½ Tablespoon Chili Flakes
- ¼ Teaspoon Crushed Pepper Corns
- ¼ Cup of Panko Breadcrumbs/Fresh Breadcrumbs
- 1 Tablespoon Dijon Mustard
- 1 Small Onion (Chopped)
- 2 Tablespoons Fresh Cilantro
- 1 Large Egg
- 500 grams Peeled Shrimps
- Salt to Taste

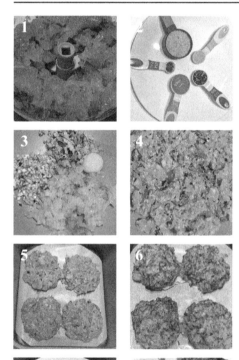

DIRECTIONS

Step 1: In a food processor, pulse the raw shrimp pieces until it looks flaky. (See Image 1)

Step 2: In a clean bowl, put together the onion, cilantro, egg, and flaky shrimps.

Step 3: Then add the chili flakes, salt, pepper, breadcrumbs, dijon mustard, and mix well.

Step 4: Divide and form into round patties. (See Image 5)

Step 5: Air fry at 360°F for 8 minutes. Flip and air fry again for 5 minutes.

Step 6: Enjoy immediately with your dip of choice and some salad!

Spinach Quiche

Prep 10 Min	Cook 20 Min	Two Servings

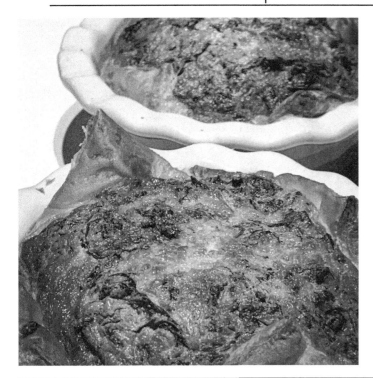

INGREDIENTS

- Puff Pastry Sheets (4 inch Squares)
- 2 Cups Frozen Spinach (Thawed and Water Squeezed Out)
- ½ Cup Grated Cheddar Cheese
- 3 Eggs
- ¼ Cup Heavy Cream
- ¼ Teaspoon Black Pepper Powder
- Salt to Taste

DIRECTIONS

Step 1: Remove the puff pastry sheets from the refrigerator about 15 minutes before preparing quiche.

Step 2: Cut the pastry sheet into 4 inches squares. If you cut it bigger if your bakeware is bigger in size.

Step 3: Place the pastry sheets into the tart pans and press down to make the cavity. (See Image 3)

Step 4: Now add the shredded cheese on top of the pastry sheets.

Step 5: Add chopped spinach on top of the pastry shredded cheese. (See Image 4)

Step 6: In a bowl, whisk together 3 eggs, cream, salt, and ground pepper. (See Image 5)

Step 7: Carefully pour egg mixture over the spinach and cheese filling. (See Image 6)

Step 8: Place the prepared quiche into the air fryer basket and air fry at 330°F for 20-25 minutes or until the egg is cooked in the center.

Step 9: Allow to cool for 5 to 10 minutes, and then carefully pop the quiche from the tart pan. Use a spatula to remove the quiche from the bottom plate of the tart pan and serve.

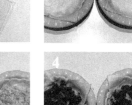

Spring Rolls (Maggie)

Prep 15 Min	Cook 20 Min	Four Servings

INGREDIENTS

- Spring Roll Wrappers (Jumbo)
- Maggie Noodles
- 2 Eggs (Optional)
- Mozzarella Cheese Sticks
- Sealing Paste (1 Tablespoon Flour + 2 Tablespoons Water)
- Oil Spray

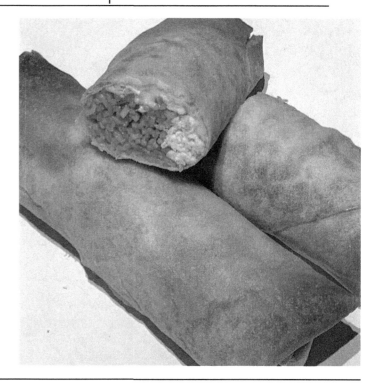

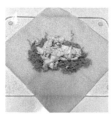
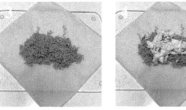

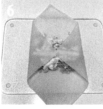

DIRECTIONS

Making maggie

Step 1: Add the maggie noodles to boiling water and cook.

Step 2: Add the maggie masala seasoning and allow it to cool.

Scrambled egg

Step 1: Beat the eggs. Place them in a medium bowl, and whisk until the yolk & whites thoroughly combines.

Step 2: Gently preheat the pan, pour in the egg mixture, sprinkle some salt and pepper and let it cook for a minute, then set it aside.

Spring Roll

Step 1: Take one jumbo spring roll wrapper and place it on your work surface. Put the maggie noodles, scrambled eggs, and cheese in the center. (See Images 3, 4, 5)

Step 2: Fold the spring roll and seal it using the sealing paste.

Step 3: Place the rolls in an air fryer basket, generously spray oil onto the spring rolls.

Step 4: Air fryer at 360°F for 15 minutes. Flip and fry again for 5 minutes.

Stuffed Eggplant

Prep 20 Min	Cook 20 Min	Two Servings

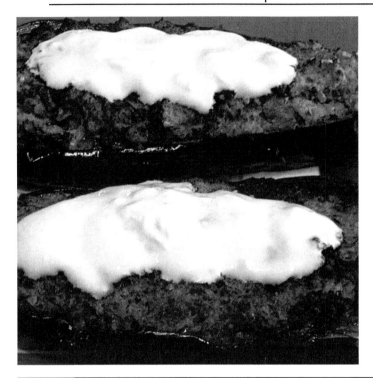

INGREDIENTS

- 1 Large Eggplant
- ¼ Cup Sliced Yellow Pepper
- ¼ Cup Sliced Green Pepper
- Half Tomato
- 2 Garlic Cloves
- ¼ Teaspoon Ground Pepper
- ½ Teaspoon Chili Flakes
- 1 Teaspoon Salt
- 1 Cup Fresh Breadcrumbs
- 2 Tablespoons Parmesan Cheese
- 2 Tablespoons Olive Oil

DIRECTIONS

Step 1: Cut the eggplant in half. Brush generous amount of olive oil onto the eggplants.

Step 2: Air fry at 350°F for 12 minutes. (See Image 3)

Step 3: To make the filling, finely chop the bell-bell-peppers, tomato, and garlic cloves. To this add ground pepper and chili flakes. Finally, mix in the fresh breadcrumbs and parmesan cheese. Mix everything very well.

Step 4: Take out the air fried eggplants, give it a few slits on top and create a cavity. (See Image 8)

Step 5: Generously top it with the filling mixture and air fry again at 350°F for 10 minutes.

Step 6: Serve with sour cream topping with rice or bread of your choice!

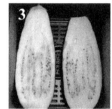
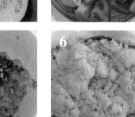

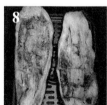
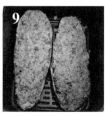
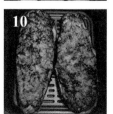

Stuffed Tomatoes

Prep 5 Min	Cook 15 Min	Four Servings

INGREDIENTS

- 4-6 Large Tomatoes
- 1 Cup Cream Cheese
- ½ Cup Shredded Cheddar Cheese
- 1 Tablespoon Dried Parsley
- ¼ Teaspoon Garlic Salt
- Panko Breadcrumbs
- Butter

DIRECTIONS

Step 1: In a bowl, add cream cheese, cheddar cheese, parsley, and garlic salt. Mix everything together and your filling is ready.

Step 2: Cut the tomatoes into halves and remove the inside seeds and pulp.

Step 3: Fill each tomatoes with the cream cheese filling.

Step 4: Coat the tomatoes with the panko breadcrumbs. (Follow as in the Images)

Step 5: Add a dollop of butter on top (you can use oil spray as well).

Step 6: Air fry at 360°F for 15 minutes or until the mixture is light golden brown.

Sweet Potato French Fries

Prep 5 Min	Cook 12 Min	Two Servings

INGREDIENTS

- 1 Large Sweet Potato
- 1 Teaspoon Crushed Black Peppercorns
- ½ Teaspoon Salt
- 1 Teaspoon Chili Flakes (Optional)
- Olive Oil Spray

DIRECTIONS

Step 1: Peel and slice the sweet potato into medium-thin slices (fries style).

Step 2: In a bowl, toss in the sweet potato along with chili flakes, crushed peppercorns, and salt. Give it a good mix.

Step 3: Spray oil generously and air fry at 360°F for 8 minutes. Remove and give it a good shake and fry again for 5 minutes.

Toasted Cheese Baguette

Prep 5 Min	Cook 5 Min	Two Servings

INGREDIENTS

- 1 Tablespoon Dried Parsley
- 3-5 Big Garlic Cloves Minced
- 6 Small Cubes of Butter (3 Tablespoons)
- Salt to Taste
- Baguette — Sliced into 6 inches Lengthwise
- Shredded Mozzarella Cheese

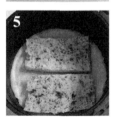 
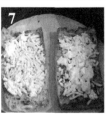 

DIRECTIONS

Step 1: Mix together the softened butter, minced garlic, salt, and dried parsley.

Step 2: Spread the mixture onto sliced baguettes.

Step 3: Add generous amount of shredded mozzarella.

Step 4: Place the baguette into your air fryer basket in a single layer.

Step 5: Air fry at 375°F for 5 minutes.

Note: If you like brown toasted cheese top like mine then air fry at 400°F for 1 minute.

Tofu/Paneer Puffs

Prep 20 Min	Cook 20 Min	Four Servings

INGREDIENTS

- Pastry Sheets (6 inches Squares)
- ¼ Cup Onion (Chopped)
- ⅓ Teaspoon Turmeric Powder
- 1 Teaspoon Coriander Powder
- 1 Teaspoon Red Chili Powder
- ½ Cup Tomatoes (Chopped)
- 2 Tablespoons Oil
- 1 Cup Grated Tofu/Paneer
- Salt to Taste

DIRECTIONS

Step 1: Heat oil in a pan and saute the onion.

Step 2: Once the onion is translucent, add in the tomatoes and the spices (turmeric, coriander, red chili powder). Give it a good mix.

Step 3: Add the grated tofu/paneer, mix it with the tomato mixture, sprinkle some salt on top and close the lid and let it cook for 5 minutes on medium to low flame.

Step 4: Now take the pastry sheet and put 2 tablespoons of stuffing on top of it and close the corners together as shown in the image. Make sure to perfectly seal it.

Step 5: Preheat the air fryer at 400°F for 3 minutes. Arrange the tofu/paneer puff inside the basket. Don't overcrowd.

Step 6: Air fry at 350°F for 15 minutes or until brown and crispy.

Tomato Carrot Soup

Prep 10 Min	Cook 15 Min	Four Servings

INGREDIENTS

- 3-4 Large Tomatoes
- 2 Large Carrots
- 3 Large Garlic Cloves
- 1 Tablespoon Olive Oil
- 1 Tablespoon Dried Thyme
- 2 Cups Chicken/Vegetable Stock
- 1 Tablespoon Butter
- 1 Maggie Masala Cube

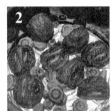

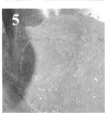
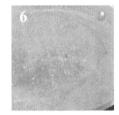

DIRECTIONS

Step 1: Wash the vegetable and pat them dry, peel and slice the carrots into 5-6 cm in thickness, cut the tomatoes into 3-4 slices.

Step 2: Put all the vegetables into the air fryer basket. Add garlic cloves and drizzle 1 tablespoon of olive oil.

Step 3: Air fry at 375°F for 10-12 minutes (take out after 10 minutes and if it still needs more roasting then cook for 2 to 3 more minutes).

Step 4: Transfer them all to a blender jar, and add the maggie masala cube and chicken/vegetable broth. Blend everything together.

Step 5: Heat butter in a deep bottom pan and add the dried thyme, saute for a minute. Then add the tomato soup mixture and bring to boil and turn off the flame.

Step 6: Garnish with fresh/dried basil.

MAIN COURSE

Baked Mac and Cheese

Prep 5 Min	Cook 30 Min	Four Servings

INGREDIENTS

- 1 Cup Shredded Cheddar Cheese
- ¼ Cup Elbow Macaroni
- ¼ Cup Velveeta Cheese
- 1 Cup Whipping Cream
- ½ Teaspoon Ground Black Pepper
- 1 Teaspoon Garlic Powder

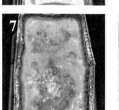

DIRECTIONS

Step 1: In a baking pan, combine elbow macaroni and whipping cream. Give it a good mix.

Step 2: Add the shredded cheddar and velveeta. Mix everything together.

Step 3: Sprinkle ground black pepper and garlic powder and mix again.

Step 4: Seal the baking pan with an aluminum foil.

Step 5: Air fry at 360°F for 20 minutes. Take out give it a good mix and air fry again at 360°F for 20 more minutes.

Step 6: For that extra cheesy feel, add 2 tablespoons of shredded cheddar on top and air fry at 400 for 3 minutes. (Optional)

Note: Don't worry if you mac and cheese appear runny after it's done cooking. As you stir it up for serving, it will thick and gooey.

BBQ Cauliflower Poppers

Prep 10 Min	Cook 18 Min	Four Servings

INGREDIENTS

- ½ Cup BBQ Sauce
- ¼ Cup Maple Syrup
- 2 Cup Cauliflower Florets (Bite Size)
- ½ Teaspoon Salt
- ¼ Teaspoon Ground Pepper
- 1 Cup All-Purpose Flour
- 1 Cup Breadcrumbs
- 1 Tablespoon Sriracha Sauce
- 1 Cup Water
- Oil Spray

DIRECTIONS

Step 1: First, combine the flour, salt, pepper, and water and make a thick batter. (See Image 2)

Step 2: Place the cauliflower florets into the flour mixture and coat the cauliflower. (See Image 3)

Step 3: Now coat them well in breadcrumbs. Make sure to cover all the sides. (See Image 4)

Step 4: Place them into the air fryer basket and spray oil generously.

Step 5: Air fry at 350°F for 15 minutes.

Step 6: **For the glaze,** in a clean bowl, mix the BBQ sauce, maple syrup, and sriracha. (See Image 6)

Step 7: Toss the air fried cauliflower popcorns into the BBQ sauce mix and coat them well.

Step 8: Air fry the BBQ sauce coated cauliflower popcorns at 375°F for 2-3 minutes.

Note: Sprinkle some sesame seeds and serve hot and crispy!

BBQ Chicken Wings

Prep 5 Min	Cook 20 Min	Four Servings

INGREDIENTS

- 1 Cup All-Purpose Flour
- 1 Teaspoon Salt
- 1 Teaspoon Paprika Powder
- ¼ Teaspoon Ground Black Pepper
- 1 Cup BBQ Sauce
- ½ Cup Maple Syrup
- 1 Tablespoon Sriracha Hot Sauce
- 15-20 Pieces of Chicken Wings (Drumette and Winglet Separated)

DIRECTIONS

Step 1: First, combine all your dry ingredients in a clean bowl/tray, all-purpose flour, salt, paprika powder, and black pepper.

Step 2: Clean and pat dry the chicken and coat them well with a flour mixture you just made.

Step 3: Place the chicken wings into the preheated air fryer and fair fry at 375°F for 15 minutes. Take out and give it a good shake and air fry again for another 10-15 minutes at same temperature.

Step 4: To make the BBQ sauce, in a big bowl, combine all the liquid ingredients (BBQ sauce, maple syrup, and sriracha hot sauce).

Step 5: Coat the air fried chicken wings with the BBQ sauce you just made. (See Image 6)

Step 6: Air fry the BBQ sauce coated chicken wings for 2-3 minutes at 400°F.

Bengali Mach (Fish) Bhaja

Prep 5 Min	Cook 20 Min	Four Servings

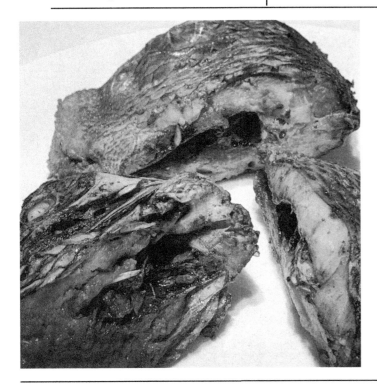

INGREDIENTS

- 1 Large Tilapia
- 2 Teaspoons Turmeric Powder
- Salt to Taste
- 1 Tablespoon Lemon Juice

DIRECTIONS

Step 1: Clean and slice the Tilapia into equal parts (or any fish that you preferred).

Step 2: Place the fish in a large bowl, sprinkle turmeric powder, and salt. Coat the fish thoroughly with the spice mix.

Step 3: Air fry at 360°F for about 15 minutes. Take it out and turn them over, and air fry again for 5-7 minutes.

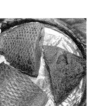
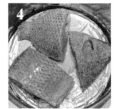
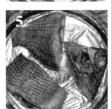
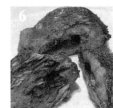

Breaded Shrimps

Prep 10 Min	Cook 10 Min	Four Servings

INGREDIENTS

- ¼ Cup Corn Starch
- ¼ Teaspoon Ground Pepper
- 1 Teaspoon Salt
- ½ All-Purpose Flour
- 1 Pound Shrimps
- Shredded Coconut (Sweetened/Unsweetened)
- 1 Cup Breadcrumbs
- Oil Spray

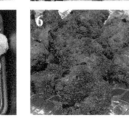

DIRECTIONS

Step 1: To make the batter, combine all-purpose flour, corn starch, ground pepper, and salt. Make a thick batter by gradually adding water. (See Image 2)

Step 2: Clean the shrimps, remove the head, and peel them. Wash and pat them dry before using.

Step 3: Take the shrimps and coat it nicely with the flour batter we just made.

Step 4: Now take out the battered shrimp and coat it evenly with breadcrumbs. (See Image 3)

Step 5: Place them in an air fryer basket and generously spray oil.

Step 6: Air fry at 375°F for 5 minutes on both sides Or until golden brown and crispy. (See Image 6)

Cauliflower Steak

Prep 5 Min	Cook 20 Min	Two Servings

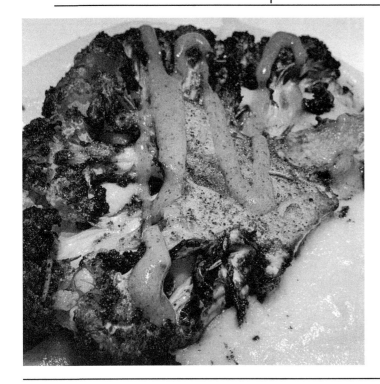

INGREDIENTS

- 2 Big and Thick Slices of Cauliflower Steak
- 1 Teaspoon Dried Rosemary
- 2 Tablespoons Avocado/Olive Oil
- 1 Teaspoon Paprika
- ½ Teaspoon Garlic Salt
- ⅛ Teaspoon Ground Black Pepper

DIRECTIONS

Step 1: In a small bowl, combine the oil, rosemary, paprika, garlic salt, and black pepper. Give it a good mix.

Step 2: Coat the cauliflower steak generously with the spice mixture on both sides. (See Image 3)

Step 3: Air fry at 350°F for 10 minutes on both sides.

Step 4: Serve with mashed potato.

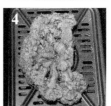

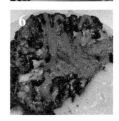

Chicken and Mushroom with More!

Prep 10 Min	Cook 30 Min	Four Servings

INGREDIENTS

- 1 Pound Chicken Thigh Pieces (Small)
- 1 Cup Potato (1 inch Cubes)
- ¼ Cup Red Onion (Chopped)
- 5-6 Mushrooms (Sliced lengthwise)
- ¼ Cup Red & Green Bell Pepper (Chopped)
- 1 Tablespoon Cumin Powder
- 1 Tablespoon Paprika
- ½ Cup Tomato Puree
- ½ Tablespoon Garlic Salt
- ½ Tablespoon Italian Seasoning Mix (Optional)
- 2 Tablespoons Oil

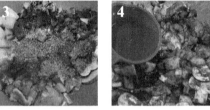
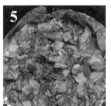  

DIRECTIONS

Step 1: In a large bowl, place the chicken, potato, mushroom, onion and bell pepper.

Step 2: Now add in all the dry spices, tomato puree, and oil. Give it a good mix so that everything is well-combined.

Step 3: Line the air fryer basket with an aluminum foil and place the chicken and mushroom mixture in it.

Step 4: Air fry at 375°F for 20 minutes. Take out, give everything a good shake and air fry again for 15 minutes.

Step 5: Serve it with tortilla or on a bread toast.

Chicken Biryani

Prep 20 Min	Cook 45 Min	Two Servings

INGREDIENTS

- 3-4 Pieces of Chicken (Drumstick)
- 1 Tablespoon Minced Garlic
- 1 Tablespoon Ginger Paste
- ½ Cup of Yogurt
- 2 Tablespoons Chicken Biryani Masala
- 1 Tablespoon Paprika
- Salt to Taste
- ¼ Cup Fried Onion
- ¼ Cup Chopped Cilantro
- 2 Cups Half-Boiled Rice
- 1 Tablespoon Chopped Mint Leaves

DIRECTIONS

Step 1: In a bowl, mix the chicken pieces with yogurt, biryani masala, paprika, minced garlic, ginger paste, fried onion, and salt. (See Images 1 and 2)

Step 2: Cover and let it marinate for an hour inside refrigerator.

Step 3: Cook rice for at least halfway through. Take one piece and break it in between fingers. It should break into 2 or 3 pieces but not get mashed. (See Image 3)

Step 4: Take a bowl that would fit in your air fryer. Put the marinated chicken in the bottom, place the rice on top of it and add some fried onion, cilantro, and mint leaves.

Step 5: Sprinkle saffron milk and kewra water on top. (Optional)

Step 6: Cover/seal it with aluminum foil and place it in the preheated air fryer, cook at 350°F for 45 minutes.

Chicken Chimichanga

Prep 20 Min	Cook 20 Min	Four Servings

INGREDIENTS

- 2-3 Cups Shredded Chicken Meat (Leftover Rotisserie)
- ¼ Cup Minced Red Onion
- ¼ Cup Mayonnaise Ketchup
- ½ Tablespoon Chili Flakes
- 4-6 Tortillas
- 1 Cup Shredded Cheddar Cheese
- Olive Oil Spray/Brush

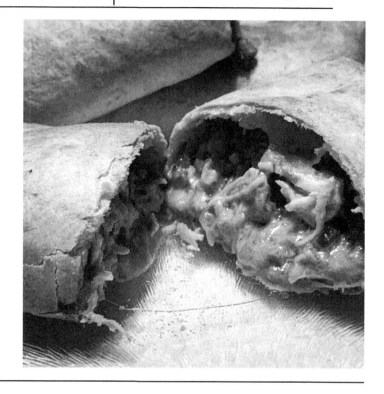

DIRECTIONS

Step 1: In a large bowl, place the shredded chicken together with the onion, mayonnaise, and chili flakes. Give it a good mix.

Step 2: On a tortilla, put at least 1-2 spoons full of the chicken mixture, add a generous amount of shredded cheddar cheese and fold the tortilla into burrito.

Step 3: Place 2-3 pieces of tortilla in the preheated air fryer and brush/spray olive oil.

Step 4: Air fry at 360°F for 10-12 minutes, or until crispy.

Chicken Corn Taquitos

Prep 10 Min	Cook 20 Min	Four Servings

INGREDIENTS

- 4-5 Pieces Boiled Chicken Drumstick
- 1 Tablespoon Paprika
- Salt to Taste
- 1 Teaspoon Cumin Powder
- ¼ Teaspoon Crushed Black Pepper Corns
- 6-8 Corn Tortilla
- Lemon Juice
- Sliced Onion
- Sliced Cabbage
- Sour Cream
- Olive Oil Spray

DIRECTIONS

Step 1: After boiling the chicken drumstick, separate the meat from the bones (you can also take left-over chicken).

Step 2: In a bowl, mix together shredded chicken, paprika, salt, crushed black pepper, and cumin powder. Give it a nice mix.

Step 3: Take corn tortilla, place 2-3 tablespoons of chicken mixture and roll them all up.

Step 4: Place at least 4-5 pieces of taquitos into the preheat air fryer and spray/brush oil.

Step 5: Air fry the taquitos at 360°F for about 12-15 minutes or until Crispy on both sides.

Step 6: Serve and Garnish with sliced cabbage, onion, and sour cream.

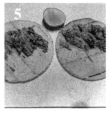

Chicken Empanadas

Prep 20 Min	Cook 20 Min	Four Servings

INGREDIENTS

- 1 Egg
- 3 Tablespoons Unsalted Butter
- 1 Cup All-Purpose Flour
- ¼ Tablespoon Salt
- ¼ Cup Minced Onion
- ½ Cup Shredded Cheddar Cheese
- 1 Cup Shredded Chicken (Leftover rotisserie)
- ¼ Cup Mayo Ketchup (Mayochup)

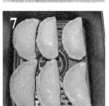

DIRECTIONS

Step 1: Take a dry and clean bowl, mix the flour with butter and salt for few minutes, or until it holds shape.

Step 2: Add egg and make a dough (no water needed). Rest the dough for at least 1 hour.

Step 3: For filling, mix onion, shredded cheese, shredded chicken, and the mayochup together.

Step 4: Knead the rested dough for few minutes, slice them into equal sized balls, and roll into small sheets.

Step 5: Place 1-2 tablespoons of the chicken filling in the middle of your dough.

Step 6: Fold and seal, just like in the given images.

Step 7: Place them in the preheated air fryer and air fry at 360°F for 20 minutes or until brown. Take out and flip them and air fry again for 5 minutes.

Chicken Fajitas

Prep 5 Min	Cook 20 Min	Four Servings

INGREDIENTS

- Green, Yellow, and Red Bell Peppers
- Sliced Onion
- 1 Tablespoon Avocado Oil
- 1 ½ Tablespoons Taco Seasoning
- 1 Pound Chicken Thighs (Cut Lengthwise)

DIRECTIONS

Step 1: Line the air fryer basket with an aluminium foil and a parchment paper.

Step 2: Add all the ingredients. Toss and mix everything together.

Step 3: Air fry at 375°F for 12 minutes. Remove and give it a good shake and air fry again for 10 minutes.

Note: Sprinkle lime juice and serve with tortilla as taco!

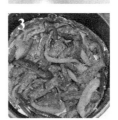

Chicken Kabab

Prep 20 Min	Cook 20 Min	Four Servings

INGREDIENTS

- 2 Chicken Breasts (Cut into Large Pieces)
- ½ Cup Yogurt
- ¼ Cup Vegetable Oil
- 2 Tablespoons Paprika
- 1 Teaspoon Cumin Powder
- 1 Teaspoon Coriander Powder
- ½ Tablespoon Kasuri Methi (Dry Fenugreek Leaves)
- 1 Tablespoon Minced Garlic
- ½ Tablespoon Grated Ginger
- ¼ Teaspoon Turmeric
- 1 Teaspoon Salt
- 4-6 Wooden Skewers

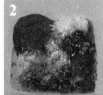

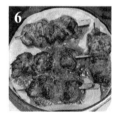

DIRECTIONS

Step 1: Cut the chicken breast pieces into 2 inches thick strips.

Step 2: In a large bowl, mix all the spices along with the yogurt and oil. Make a thick marinate.

Step 3: Add the chicken pieces and marinate for at least 30 minutes or even better, overnight (Cover with plastic wrap and put in the refrigerator).

Step 4: Thread onto the skewers and air fry at 375°F for 10 minutes on each side.

Note: Sprinkle lemon juice and serve hot!

Chicken Lasagna

Prep 20 Min	Cook 20 Min	Four Servings

INGREDIENTS

- 1 Tablespoon Cooking Oil
- 1 Pound Minced Chicken
- 1 Cup Onion (Chopped)
- 1 Cup Green Bell Pepper (Chopped)
- 2 Tablespoons Chili (Seasoning mix)
- ¼ Cup Tomato Sauce/Pure
- 6-8 No Boil (Oven Ready) Lasagna Sheets
- 1 Cup Shredded Cheese
- 1 Cup Bechamel Sauce (You Can Take Marinara Sauce as well)
- Salt to Taste

DIRECTIONS

Lasagna Meat Filling

Step 1: Heat 1 tablespoon oil in a pan and add ground chicken, onion, and bell pepper. Cook for at least 5-7 minutes.

Step 2: Add the seasoning mix and tomato sauce and cook with lid on for 10-15 minutes on high flame.

Step 3: Your Meat filling is now ready.

To Be Continued ...

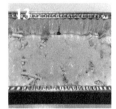

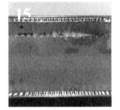

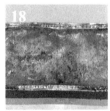

Making of Lasagna:

Step 4: Take a baking pan that will fit in your air fryer.

Step 5: Spread bechamel sauce, then a layer of chicken, then lasagna sheets, and top with shredded cheese. (Follow Images 10→11→12)

Step 6: Repeat step 2 until you have run out of ingredients. Make sure your last layer is a cheese layer.

Step 7: Seal your lasagna pan with a foil paper. Air fryer for 40-45 minutes at 350°F.

Chicken Manchurian Gravy

Prep 20 Min	Cook 20 Min	Four Servings

INGREDIENTS

- 1 Pound Breast/Thighs (Cut into Cubes)
- 1 Tablespoon Soy Sauce
- 1 Tablespoon Garlic Salt
- 1 Teaspoon Paprika Powder
- ¼ Teaspoon Ground Black Pepper
- ¼ Cup Corn Starch
- ¼ Cup All-Purpose Flour
- 1 Cup Minced Onions
- 2 Tablespoons Minced Ginger-Garlic
- 5-6 Curry Leaves (Optional)
- ¼ Cup Tomato Ketchup
- 1 Tablespoon Schezwan Sauce/Chutney
- ½ Chili Flakes (Optional)
- 2 Tablespoons Soy Sauce (for Gravy)
- Oil Spray
- 2 Tablespoons Cooking Oil (for Gravy)

DIRECTIONS

Frying the Chicken:

Step 1: Take chicken pieces in a bowl and add in soy sauce, garlic salt, paprika, black pepper powder along with all-purpose flour and corn starch. Mix everything together. (See Images 1 to 6)

Step 2: Place the chicken pieces in a preheated air fryer and air fry them at 360°F for 15 minutes. Take them out, flip them and air fry again at 360°F for 7-10 minutes.

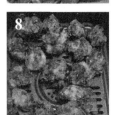

To Be Continued ...

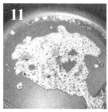 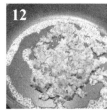

Making of the Manchurian Gravy:

Step 3: Prepare the sauce in a small bowl, mix tomato sauce, schezwan chutney, soya sauce, and chili flakes. Set aside.

Step 4: In a preheated pan/wok, add cooking oil. Add minced ginger and garlic along with a few curry leaves. Once the ginger-garlic browns up, add in the minced onion and fry for few minutes.

Step 5: Now pour the sauce mixture that you just made. Cook the mixture for 3-5 minutes on high.

Step 6: Once it's boiling, add the fried chicken pieces and mix them all together.

Step 7: If you want thick gravy, then add in 2 tablespoons corn starch mixed in ¼ cup water and cook for 5 minutes.

Chicken Meat Balls Gravy

Prep 10 Min	Cook 20 Min	Four Servings

INGREDIENTS

- 1 lb Chicken Breasts
- 1 Onion Chopped
- 2-3 Garlic Cloves
- ¼ Cup Parmesan Cheese
- 1 Teaspoon Cumin Powder
- 1 Teaspoon Paprika
- 1 Cup Marinara Sauce
- ¼ Cup Mozzarella Cheese
- Salt to Taste

DIRECTIONS

Step 1: In a food processor, blend together the chicken breast pieces, onion, garlic cloves, cumin powder, paprika, parmesan cheese and salt to taste.

Step 2: Transfer the mixture to a larger bowl and make meat balls.

Step 3: Air fry the chicken meat balls at 400°F for about 3-5 minutes.

Step 4: Now coat the meatballs with marinara sauce and the mozzarella cheese.

Step 5: Cover with foil paper and air fry at 375°F for 20 minutes.

Chicken Meatloaf

Prep 10 Min	Cook 45 Min	Six Servings

INGREDIENTS

- ½ Cup Minced Onions
- 4-5 Garlic Cloves (Minced)
- 1 Egg
- ½ Cup Carrot and Green Bell Pepper (Chopped)
- ¼ Cup Breadcrumbs
- 2 Tablespoons Grated Parmesan
- 1 Teaspoon Cumin Powder
- 1 Teaspoon Poultry Seasoning
- 1 Pound Ground Chicken
- Salt to Taste
- Fried Onion (Optional)

DIRECTIONS

Step 1: First, using blender chop up the garlic, onion, carrots, and bell pepper.

Step 2: In a large bowl, mix together the chopped veggies, spices, egg, ground meat, breadcrumbs, parmesan, and salt.

Step 3: Mix everything together. (See Image 4)

Step 4: Pour the mixture into a tin molding pan.

Step 5: It is optional but you can sprinkle some fried onion on top before placing it in the preheated air fryer.

Step 6: Air fry at 350°F for 45 minutes.

Chicken Pie

Prep 20 Min	Cook 40 Min	Four Servings

INGREDIENTS

- ¼ Cup Frozen Peas & Carrot Mix
- ¼ Cup Chopped Celery
- 2 Tablespoons Bell Pepper Chopped
- 1 Small Red Onion Chopped
- 1½ Cup Ground Chicken
- 1 Tablespoon Minced Garlic
- 1 Tablespoon All-Purpose Flour
- 2 Cups Chicken Stock
- ½ Teaspoon Dried Thyme
- Salt to Taste
- ½ Cup Whipping Cream
- 1 Tablespoon Cooking Oil
- Store Bought Pie Dough/Sheets

DIRECTIONS

Step 1: In a preheated pan, add in the garlic, cook until golden brown and then put all the veggies in the pan and saute for 5 minutes.

Step 2: Add flour and mix for about a minute.

Step 3: Pour first cup of the chicken stock into the pan and mix.

Step 4: Once it starts to boil add the ground chicken into the pan and mix.

Step 5: Add thyme and the other cup of the chicken stock, season with salt, and cook for 5 minutes.

Step 6: After 5 minutes add the cream and cook until it reduces the excess liquid and becomes thick in consistency.

Step 7: Take the dough, roll it into sheet and then place it in a pie pot.

Step 8: Now fill the pot with the chicken mix, don't overfill.

Step 9: Take the second pie sheet and cover the top portion of the pie and seal it using a fork.

Step 10: Air fry at 350°F for 40 minutes or until it is golden brown.

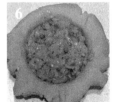

Coconut Shrimp

Prep 10 Min	Cook 12 Min	Four Servings

INGREDIENTS

- 1 Cup All-Purpose Flour
- ¼ Cup Corn Starch
- ¼ Teaspoon Ground Black Pepper
- 1 Teaspoon Salt
- Shrimps (25-30)
- 1 Cup Shredded Coconut (Sweetened/ Unsweetened)

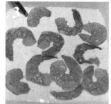
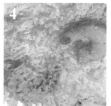

DIRECTIONS

Step 1: First, to make the batter, mix all-purpose flour, corn starch, pepper powder, and salt. Add water and make a batter like consistency. (See Image 2)

Step 2: Clean the shrimps, remove the head and peel them. Wash and pat-dry.

Step 3: Take the shrimps and put them into the batter, make sure to perfectly coat them.

Step 4: Now coat them with shredded coconut.

Step 5: Air fry at 375°F for at least 6 minutes on both sides. Don't overcrowd the air fryer for them to be nicely cooked.

Step 6: Serve them while hot and enjoy them with your preferred dipping sauce!

Cream Cheese Stuffed Salmon

Prep 10 Min	Cook 15 Min	Two Servings

INGREDIENTS

- 2 Salmon Pieces
- 1 Teaspoon Olive Oil
- ½ Tablespoon Dried Parsley
- ½ Teaspoon Garlic Salt
- 1 Teaspoon Paprika
- ½ Cup Cream Cheese

DIRECTIONS

Step 1: Clean and pat dry the salmon, cut on the side to create a pouch. (See Image 4)

Step 2: In a bowl, mix the cream cheese, dried parsley, and garlic salt together.

Step 3: Put a generous amount of filling into the salmon pouch.

Step 4: Drizzle olive oil and sprinkle some paprika on top.

Step 5: Seal the foil paper. (See Image 7)

Step 6: Air fry at 375°F for 12-15 minutes.

Note: For juicy and moist salmon, cook it sealed in an aluminum foil lined with parchment paper.

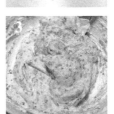

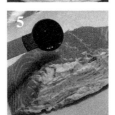

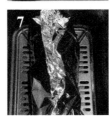

Fish Cutlet

Prep 20 Min	Cook 20 Min	Four Servings

INGREDIENTS

- 2 Basa/Cod Fish Fillets
- ½ Teaspoon Black Pepper Powder
- 1 Tablespoon Lemon Juice
- 2 Large Eggs
- ½ Cup All-Purpose Flour
- 1 Cup Breadcrumbs
- Salt to Taste
- Oil Spray

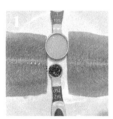

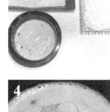
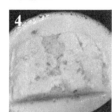

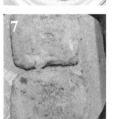
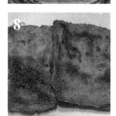

DIRECTIONS

Step 1: Marinate the fish fillet with black pepper powder and lemon juice for at least 15 minutes. (See Image 1)

Step 2: Add salt to the breadcrumbs mixture (you can add other spices of your choice too).

Making the Cutlet

Step 3: Coat the fist fillet with all-purpose flour. (See Image 3)

Step 4: Now dip the flour-coated fillet into the beaten egg mixture. (See Image 4)

Step 5: Lastly, coat it very well with breadcrumbs. (See Image 5)

Step 6: Spray oil generously and air fry at 360°F for 15 minutes. Take out, flip and cook again for 10 minutes.

Note: Serve hot with tartar sauce!

Garlic Butter Roasted Salmon

Prep 5 Min	Cook 12 Min	Two Servings

INGREDIENTS

- Salmon Fillet
- 1 Tablespoon Dried Parsley
- 3-5 Big Garlic Cloves Minced
- 6 Small Cubes of Butter (3 Tablespoons)
- Salt to Taste

DIRECTIONS

Step 1: Mix together the softened butter, minced garlic, salt, and dried parsley.

Step 2: Take a big sheet of foil paper and place a parchment on top of it. Now put the salmon fillet on top of the parchment paper.

Step 3: Spread the garlic-butter mixture on to the salmon generously on all three sides.

Step 4: Seal the buttered salmon fillet and place in the preheated air fryer. (See Image 6)

Step 5: Air fry at 375°F for 12 minutes.

Note: Depending on the thickness of the salmon, the timing may vary.

Garlic Butter Shrimp

Prep 5 Min	Cook 12 Min	Four Servings

INGREDIENTS

- 1 Pound Peeled Shrimps
- ½ Tablespoon Chili Flakes
- ½ Teaspoon Italian Seasoning
- ¼ Teaspoon Black Pepper Powder
- 1 Tablespoon Minced Garlic
- ¼ Teaspoon Salt
- 1 Tablespoon Melted Butter

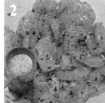
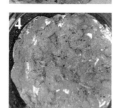
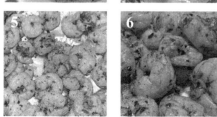

DIRECTIONS

Step 1: In a bowl place the peeled, clean, and pat-dried shrimps.

Step 2: Add in the chili flakes, Italian seasoning, black pepper, minced garlic, salt, and melted butter.

Step 3: Give it a good mix and preheat the air fryer.

Step 4: Line the air fryer basket with aluminum foil. Make it a boat shape (see image). This will prevent the butter from escaping and it will also help make the shrimp juicy.

Step 5: Put the spiced shrimps into the aluminium boat.

Step 6: Air fry at 375°F for 10 minutes. Take out give it a good shake and air fry again at 400°F for 2 minutes.

Note: This recipe goes so well with grits. Yumm!

Garlic Parmesan Chicken Wings

Prep 10 Min	Cook 20 Min	Four Servings

INGREDIENTS

- 1 Tablespoon Avocado Oil
- ½ Tablespoon Chili Flakes
- ¼ Cup Parmesan Cheese
- ½ Tablespoon Onion Powder
- 1 Tablespoon Garlic Powder
- ½ Teaspoon Pepper Powder
- 1 Tablespoon Corn Starch
- 2 Pound Chicken Wings (wash and pat dry)
- Salt to Taste

DIRECTIONS

Step 1: Preheat the air fryer to 400°F.

Step 2: Toss chicken wings with chili flakes, garlic powder, onion powder, pepper powder, and salt in a bowl until evenly coated.

Step 3: Now add corn starch and parmesan cheese and mix thoroughly.

Step 4: Place wings in a single layer in the air fryer basket, working in batches as needed.

Step 5: Air fry at 375°F for 12 minutes. Take out, give it a good shake and air fry again for 10 minutes or until the outside is crispy.

Gobi Manchurian (Pakoda)

Prep 20 Min	Cook 20 Min	Four Servings

INGREDIENTS

For Cauliflower Manchurian Florets

- 15-20 Cauliflower Florets (Wash and Pat Dry)
- 1 Cup All-Purpose Flour
- ¼ Cup Corn Starch
- ½ Tablespoon Paprika (Chili Powder)
- 1 Teaspoon Garlic Salt
- 1 Tablespoon Cumin Powder
- ¼ Teaspoon Turmeric Powder
- Oil Spray

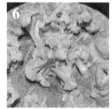

DIRECTIONS

Cauliflower Bites

Step 1: In a bog bowl, mix everything together by adding water gradually. Make a thick batter.

Step 2: Coat the cauliflower florets with the batter.

Step 3: Place the florets in the air fryer basket in a single layer and spray oil generously.

Step 4: Air fry at 350°F for 10 minutes. Take out, flip and fry again for 8 minutes or until crispy (add a minute or two if needed).

Step 5: While the cauliflower is getting air fried, prepare the Manchurian sauce.

To Be Continued ...

Gobi Manchurian (Sauce/Gravy)

Prep 10 Min	Cook 10 Min	Four Servings

INGREDIENTS

For the Manchurian Sauce

- Olive Oil
- 2 Whole Dried Red Chili
- 6-8 Curry Leaves
- 1 Tablespoon Soy Sauce
- 2 Tablespoons Ginger-Garlic (Minced/Paste)
- ¼ Cup Red Onion (Chopped)
- 1 Tablespoon Ketchup
- 1 Tablespoon Schezwan Chutney (Store Bought)
- 1 Cup Water
- 2 Tablespoons Corn Starch (Mix with Water and Use)
- 2 Tablespoons Fresh Cilantro

DIRECTIONS

Step 1: Heat oil in a pan and add the dried red chili, minced garlic, and onion. Saute for 2 to 3 minutes.

Step 2: Now add soy sauce, schezwan chutney, ketchup, and water. Cook for 2 to 3 minutes.

Step 3: Now add in the corn starch water mixture and cook for 2 minutes.

Step 4: Now add the air-fried cauliflower to the pan and toss with the manchurian sauce. Garnish with chopped fresh cilantro.

Imitation Crab Cake

Prep 10 Min	Cook 20 Min	Four Servings

INGREDIENTS

- 1 Pound Imitation Crab Meat
- 1 Egg
- ¼ Cup Mayonnaise
- ½ Cup Panko Breadcrumbs
- 1 Tablespoon Dijon Mustard
- ½ Tablespoon Sriracha Hot Sauce
- ½ Tablespoon Soy Sauce
- ¼ Teaspoon Ground Black Pepper

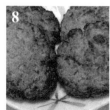

DIRECTIONS

Step 1: In a food processor, chop the crab meat coarsely.

Step 2: In a bowl add the egg, mayonnaise, Dijon mustard, sriracha, soy sauce, and ground black pepper. Give everything a good mix.

Step 3: Add the chopped-up crab meat and panko breadcrumbs. Mix everything together. (See Image 5)

Step 4: Keep aside for at least 30 minutes (this will help in the binding as the panko breadcrumbs will soften up).

Step 5: Form into patties of your choice.

Step 6: Air fry at 350°F for 15 minutes. Take out, flip and air fry again for 8-10 minutes.

Note: You do not need oil for this recipe as the mayonnaise already has oil in it which will be released during the sir frying process.

Lemon Pepper Chicken Thighs

Prep 10 Min	Cook 30 Min	Six Servings

INGREDIENTS

- ¼ Cup Olive Oil
- 1 Tablespoon Garlic Salt
- 1 Tablespoon Paprika Powder
- 1 Tablespoon Italian Seasoning
- 2 Tablespoons Lemon Pepper Seasoning
- 5-6 Pieces Chicken Thighs with Skin (Any Part is Okay)

DIRECTIONS

Step 1: First, mix together all the dry ingredients in olive oil.

Step 2: Place the chicken pieces into air fryer basket.

Step 3: Brush the spice mixture generously on the chicken pieces. Flip and add more of the mixture. Coat the chicken pieces nicely with the spice mixture.

Step 4: Air fry at 375°F for 15 minutes. Take out Flip and air fry again for 15 minutes.

Step 5: To make the skin extra crispy, air fry at 400°F for 2 minutes before serving.

Note: Don't forget to line the air fryer basket with aluminum foil and a parchment paper. This will make the cleaning much easier and faster.

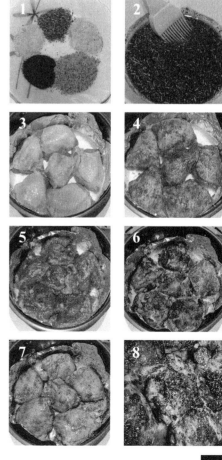

Paneer/Tofu Tikka

Prep 10 Min	Cook 15 Min	Four Servings

INGREDIENTS

- 12-15 Paneer/Tofu Cubes (3 inches Squares)
- ⅓ Cup Yogurt
- 1 Tablespoon Ginger-Garlic Paste/Grated
- 1 Tablespoon Paprika
- ¼ Teaspoon Turmeric Powder
- 1 Teaspoon Dried Fenugreek Leaves
- ½ Tablespoon Cumin Powder
- ½ Tablespoon Coriander Powder
- 1 Tablespoon Roasted Gram Flour
- Green Bell Pepper (3 inches Cubes)
- Onion (3 inches Cubes)
- Tomatoes (3 inches Cubes)
- Salt to Taste
- ¼ Cup Vegetable Oil
- 6-8 Wooden Skewers

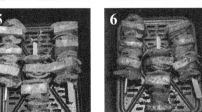

DIRECTIONS

Step 1: In a mixing bowl, add the oil, yogurt, ginger-garlic paste, roasted gram flour, and all the spices. Mix them very well with the help of a whisk.

Step 2: Now add the paneer cubes first and cost it thoroughly with the marinate mixture.

Step 3: Now add the veggies and coat them too.

Step 4: Thread into skewers (tomato-paneer-onion-green bell pepper).

Step 5: Air fry at 375°F for 8 minutes. Turn them and air fry again for 8 more minutes.

Panko Crusted Basa/Cod

Prep 20 Min	Cook 20 Min	Four Servings

INGREDIENTS

- 2 Basa/Cod
- Dollops of Butter
- 2 Cups Panko Breadcrumbs
- ¼ Cup Honey Mustard Sauce

DIRECTIONS

Step 1: Wash the fish fillets and pat it dry using the paper towels.

Step 2: Brush generous amount of honey mustard and coat the fish fillets on both sides. (See Image 2)

Step 3: Now coat fish fillets with panko breadcrumbs. (See Image 3)

Step 4: Place the fish fillets in an air fryer basket lined with parchment paper.

Step 5: Put a dollop or two of butter on top. (See Image 5)

Step 6: Air fry at 375°F for 15 minutes. Flip and air fry again on the other side for another 15 minutes or until crispy.

Note: You can also use oil spray instead of butter.

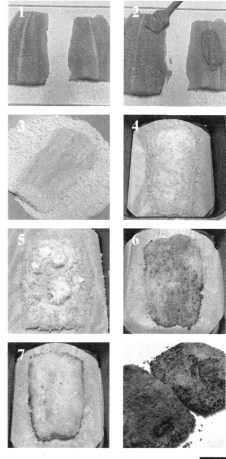

Potato Chicken Drumstick

Prep 20 Min	Cook 15 Min	Four Servings

INGREDIENTS

- 4 Chicken Leg Pieces
- 2-3 Pieces Bay Leaves
- 1 Teaspoon Chili Flakes
- ¼ Teaspoon Pepper
- 1 Teaspoon Garlic Salt
- ¼ Teaspoon Black Pepper Powder
- ¼ Cup Cheddar Cheese
- 1 Cup Boiled Mashed Potato
- 2 Large Eggs (Beaten with 1 Tablespoon of Water)
- 1 Cup Breadcrumbs
- Oil Spray

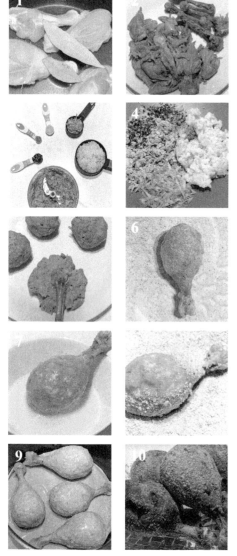

DIRECTIONS

Step 1: Boil the chicken with the bay leaf for until the meat is well cooked.

Step 2: Separate the meat from the bones, then use a hand blender grind the boiled chicken. (See Images 2 and 3)

Step 3: In a clean bowl, toss all the ingredients, chicken, cheddar cheese, mashed potato, chili flakes, black pepper, and garlic salt. Mix everything together to form a dough.

Step 4: Separate them into equal sizes, take the leftover bones from the previous step and shape them into a perfect looking drumstick.

Step 5: Roll them into the flour, then the egg mixture, and then coat with breadcrumbs.

Step 6: Place them in a preheated air fryer basket, spray oil generously and air fry them at 375°F for 10-12 minutes until golden brown and crispy.

Roasted Chicken Legs

Prep 5 Min	Cook 30 Min	Two Servings

INGREDIENTS

- 2 Whole Chicken Leg Pieces
- 1 Tablespoon Curry Powder
- 1 Tablespoon Onion Powder
- 1 Tablespoon Garlic Salt
- 1 Tablespoon Paprika
- ½ Tablespoon Dried Oregano
- 1 Teaspoon Black Pepper Powder
- Oil Spray (Optional)

DIRECTIONS

Step 1: Clean and pat dry the chicken leg pieces. Put 3 small cuts on the skin. (See Image 3)

Step 2: In a clean bowl, mix all the dry ingredients.

Step 3: Rub the spice mixture generously on both sides of the chicken leg pieces.

Step 4: Spray oil and rub again.

Step 5: Wrap and seal the chicken pieces using foil before placing it in the air fryer (see image 6). This helps make the chicken juicy.

Step 6: Air fry at 375°F for 25 minutes. Take out, open the foil paper and spray/brush some oil.

Step 7: Air fry again at 375°F for 5 minutes for that crispy skin.

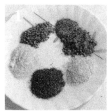

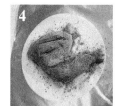

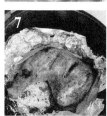
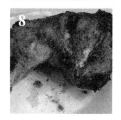

Roasted Whole Chicken

Prep 10 Min	Cook 60 Min	Six Servings

INGREDIENTS

- 1 Whole Chicken
- 2 Tablespoons Dried Rosemary
- 2 Tablespoons Dried Thyme
- 2 Tablespoons Oregano
- 1 Tablespoon Ground Black Pepper
- 2 Tablespoons Garlic Salt
- 2 Tablespoons Paprika
- ¼ Cup Olive Oil

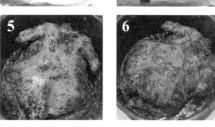

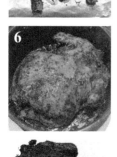

DIRECTIONS

Step 1: In a bowl, mix all the ingredients, rosemary, thyme, oregano, ground pepper, garlic salt, paprika, and olive oil.

Step 2: Take whole chicken (washed and pat dried).

Step 3: Generously spread the spice mixture you just made. Make sure to cover the entire chicken (both sides).

Step 4: Place the chicken into the preheated air fryer (breast side down).

Step 5: Air fry at 375°F for 30 minutes.

Step 6: Take it out, flip the chicken and air fry again for 30 minutes. Check every 15 minutes.

Step 7: For that extra crispy skin, air fry the chicken at 400°F for 2-3 minutes before serving.

Note: Serve with mashed potatoes and garlic toast!

Simple Veggie Pizza

Prep 20 Min	Cook 30 Min	Four Servings

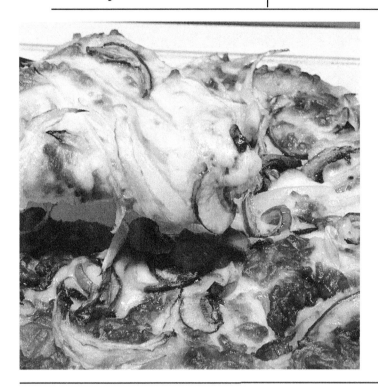

INGREDIENTS

- 2 Cups All-Purpose Flour
- 1 Teaspoon Salt
- ½ Tablespoon Brown Sugar
- 1 Tablespoon Active Dry Yeast
- 2 Tablespoons Olive Oil
- 1 Cup Milk
- Sliced Bell Pepper
- Sliced White Onion
- 3-4 Pieces Sliced Mushrooms
- ½ Cup Pizza Sauce
- 1 Cup Shredded Mozzarella Cheese

DIRECTIONS

Making of Pizza Dough

Step 1: Warm the milk (DO NOT BOIL), add brown sugar and active dry yeast. Mix and let it sit for 5 minutes. Yeast is activated when you see froth on top of the milk mixture. (See Image 5)

Step 2: In a mixing bowl, add flour, salt, and olive oil. Give it a good mix for about 2 to 3 minutes (until it loosely holds shape).

Step 3: Now add the activated yeast milk to the flour mixture and prepare a smooth and soft dough. Knead it for at least 7 to 10 minutes on low. If you are using hand then knead it for 5 minutes or until it appears smooth. (See Image 7)

Step 4: Once the dough is done, cover with a damp cloth/plastic wrap and let it rise in a warm place for 1.5 hours.

To Be Continued ...

Making of Pizza

Step 5: Take out the proofed pizza dough and knead it for a minute to release the air from inside.

Step 6: Roll it into 2 inches thick round pizza base. (See Image 10)

Step 7: Place the rolled dough on an air fryer basket. (See Image 11)

Step 8: Spread generous amount of pizza sauce on the rolled dough.

Step 9: Add a generous amount of shredded mozzarella on top of the sauce. (Depends on how cheesy you want your pizza to be.)

Step 10: And now for the toppings, add the bell peppers, onion, and mushrooms. (You can use any topping of your choice.)

Step 11: Air fry at 360°F for 12 minutes.

Step 12: Take it out, cover the top of the pizza with an aluminium foil (This will prevent the top from burning). Air fry again at 375°F for 15 minutes.

Note: Feel free to use store-bought pizza dough for faster cooking.

Sorshe Hilsha (Ilish) Bhapa (Bong Style)

Prep 20 Min	Cook 40 Min	Three Servings

INGREDIENTS

- 3-6 Pieces Ilish Mach (Hilsa Fish)
- ½ Teaspoon Salt
- 1 Green Chili
- 2 Tablespoons Poppy Seeds
- 1 Tablespoon Pure Mustard Oil
- 4 Tablespoons Black Mustard Seeds
- Salt to Taste

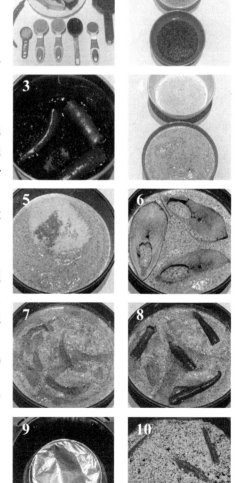

DIRECTIONS

Step 1: In two small bowls, separately soak the mustard seeds and poppy seeds in water for 30 minutes. (4 tablespoons water for mustard seeds and 2 tablespoons of water for poppy seeds).

Step 2: After 30 minutes, blend the mustard seeds along with salt and green chili. Make a smooth paste.

Step 3: Also blend the poppy seeds and make a smooth paste.

Step 4: Take an 8 inch air fryer pan and mix together the mustard seeds paste, poppy seeds paste, and turmeric powder. Give it a good mix. Add 4 to 5 tablespoons of water and mix.

Step 5: Drizzle mustard oil over the top with green chili (slit into two).

Step 6: Seal the pan with an aluminium foil and air fry at 350°F for 40 minutes.

Stuffed Chicken Breast

Prep 10 Min	Cook 30 Min	Four Servings

INGREDIENTS

- ½ Cup Soy Sauce
- ⅓ Cup Cream Cheese
- Sliced Jalapenos
- Shredded Cheddar Cheese
- ½ Cup Flour
- 1 Large Egg
- 1 Cup Breadcrumbs
- 2 Chicken Breast Pieces

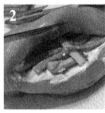

DIRECTIONS

Step 1: Clean and pat dry the chicken breast, make a pouch cut on the side where you can put the filling later.

Step 2: Marinate the chicken breast in soya sauce for 15-30 minutes.

Step 3: Start filling the chicken by generously spreading cream cheese on the inside.

Step 4: Now add the jalapenos and generous amount of shredded cheddar cheese. (See Images 2 and 3)

Step 5: Now coat the stuffed breast pieces with flour, then dip in egg mixture, and finally coat with breadcrumbs. (See Images 4 to 6)

Step 6: Place it in the preheated air fryer, air fry at 360°F for 25 minutes or until golden brown.

Note: Line the air fryer basket with parchment paper because the cheese will ooze out while frying and that's OK :)

Sweet Potato Chat (Oh! So Indian)

Prep 20 Min	Cook 10 Min	Four Servings

INGREDIENTS

- 1 Large Sweet Potato (2 Cups when Cut into Cubes)
- 1 Teaspoon Olive Oil
- Chili Flakes (Optional)
- ¼ Cup Chopped Onion
- ¼ Cup Beaten Yogurt
- ¼ Cup Chopped Tomatoes
- Indian Tamarind Chutney
- Indian Green Chutney
- 1 Teaspoon Chat Masala
- Indian Sev to Garnish

DIRECTIONS

Step 1: Cut the sweet potatoes into 2 inches cubes.

Step 2: In a clean bowl, toss the sweet potatoes and season them with olive oil and chili flakes.

Step 3: Air fryer at 350°F for 5 minutes. Remove and give it a good shake and air fry again for 5 minutes.

Making of Chat

Step 1: Finely chop the onion and tomatoes.

Step 2: Take the roasted sweet potato cubes on a plate.

Step 3: First, add the beaten yogurt, then the green chutney, and tamarind chutney. (See Images 5, 6, and 7)

Step 4: Then sprinkle the chopped onions and tomatoes on top.

Step 5: Finally, sprinkle chat masala and sev before serving.

Note: Serve immediately after making the chat! Sweet potatoes have a tendency to go soggy fast.

Tofu/Paneer Tacos

Prep 10 Min	Cook 16 Min	Four Servings

INGREDIENTS

- Extra Firm Tofu/Paneer, 1 Block (Cut into 2 inches Cubes)
- Tortillas (Flour/Corn)
- Greek Yogurt Spread
- 1 Cup Onion (Chopped into 2 inch Cubes)
- 1 Tablespoon Garlic (Grated/Minced)
- ½ Cup Red Bell Peppers (Chopped into 2 inch Cubes)
- ½ Cup Green Bell Peppers (Chopped into 2 inch Cubes)
- 1 Tablespoon Oil
- 1 Teaspoon Cumin Powder
- ¼ Teaspoon Turmeric
- ½ Teaspoon Black Pepper Powder
- ½ Tablespoon Paprika

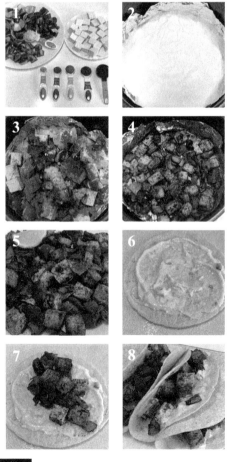

DIRECTIONS

Step 1: Press extra-firm tofu with some heavy objects for at least 30 minutes. This will drain the excess moisture. Then cut the tofu into cubes.

Step 2: Line the air fryer basket with aluminum foil and place parchment paper on top of the aluminum foil. (See Image 2)

Step 3: Put the Tofu, onion, garlic, red and green bell peppers, oil, and all the spices together and give it a good mix so that everything is nicely coated with the spice mix.

Step 4: Air fry at 350°F for 10 minutes. Remove and give it a good shake and air fry again for 5-6 minutes.

Step 5: Microwave the tortilla for 30 seconds.

Step 6: Spread the 'Greek yogurt spread' on the warm tortillas, then add the tofu fajitas and serve (you can also add other toppings of your choice).

Note: You can replace the spices with 2 tablespoons of taco seasoning!

Tomato Garlic Feta Pasta

Prep 5 Min	Cook 15 Min	Four Servings

INGREDIENTS

- 1 Pint Cherry Tomatoes (Approximately 25)
- ½ Block Feta Cheese (Approximately 1 Cup)
- 1 Teaspoon Italian Seasoning
- ½ Teaspoon Ground Black Pepper
- 1 Cup Pasta of Choice
- 2½ Tablespoons Olive Oil
- 3 Large Garlic Cloves

DIRECTIONS

Step 1: In a baking pan, toss the whole cherry tomatoes, place block of feta in the middle, garlic cloves, and season with Italian seasoning and ground black pepper. (See Images 2 and 3)

Step 2: Drizzle the oil all over the garlic-tomato-feta mix.

Step 3: Air fry at 375°F for 15 minutes.

Step 4: Meanwhile, boil a large pot of generously salted water over high heat. Add Pasta and cook until it's done. Drain and set aside.

Step 5: Take out the grilled Garlic-Tomato-Feta from the air fryer. Use the back of spoon to Smash the tomatoes, garlic and feta into a smooth and creamy sauce. (See Image 5)

Step 6: Toss in pasta until evenly coated. Taste and adjust with salt and pepper as needed.

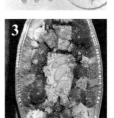
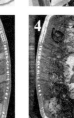
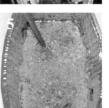
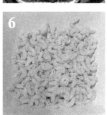
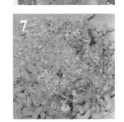

DESSERT

Air Fried Oreo

Prep 5 Min	Cook 9 Min	Four Servings

INGREDIENTS

- Oreo's 8-10 Pieces (Store Bought)
- Crescents Croissants Sheets

DIRECTIONS

Step 1: Cut the sheets of Crescents Croissants into triangles as per the direction.

Step 2: Place the cookie at the broad corner of the croissants sheets triangle.

Step 3: Wrap around the oreo cookie with the croissant's dough.

Step 4: Line the basket of the air fryer with a parchment piece. Place oreo balls into the air fryer. Arrange the cookies on the parchment in a single layer without touching (make sure to place a cookie on each of the four corners so the parchment doesn't fly up during cooking).

Step 5: Air fry at 350°F for 7 to 9 minutes or until the croissant's dough is golden brown and puffed.

Step 6: Sprinkle powdered sugar and Enjoy!

Baked Rasgulla

Prep 10 Min	Cook 40 Min	Four Servings

INGREDIENTS

- Canned/Fresh Rasgulla (Squeeze Out The Syrup)
- 1 Cup Full Fat Milk
- 1 Cup Khoya
- ½ Cup Condensed Milk
- 2 Crushed Cardamom Pods
- Saffron
- Almonds to Garnish

DIRECTIONS

Step 1: In a microwave safe bowl, add milk, khoya, condensed milk, and crushed cardamom. Give it a good mix.

Step 2: Microwave the mixture for 5 minutes.

Step 3: In a baking dish arrange the rasgullas.

Step 4: Pour the rabdi mixture that you just made. (See Image 6)

Step 5: Sprinkle some saffron on top.

Step 6: Seal the bakeware with aluminium foil and air fry at 350°F for 40 minutes.

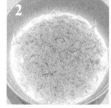

Banana-Walnut Choco Chips Muffin

Prep 10 Min	Cook 15 Min	Six Servings

INGREDIENTS

- 1 Ripe Banana
- ½ Cup Brown Sugar
- 1 Egg
- 3 Tablespoons Yogurt
- 1 Tablespoon Pure Vanilla Extract
- Pinch of Salt
- 1 Tablespoon Baking Powder
- 1½ Cups All-Purpose Flour
- ¼ Cup Semisweet Chocolate Chips
- ¼ Cup Walnuts (Crushed)

DIRECTIONS

Step 1: In a large bowl, mash the ripe banana mixture until it is smooth.

Step 2: Add in the brown sugar, egg, yogurt, and vanilla extract and mix until everything is incorporated.

Step 3: Using a strainer, sift the all-purpose flour and baking powder. Mix everything together into a smooth thick batter consistency.

Step 4: Add the crushed walnuts and chocolate chips to the mixture.

Step 5: Fill your muffin tin/muffin cups about 2/3 the way full. Set the muffin cups into the air fryer, and set the temperature to 345°F for 12 minutes.

Note: Cover the muffins with a sheet of aluminum foil to avoid burning the crust.

Blueberry Pie

Prep 5 Min	Cook 20 Min	Two Servings

INGREDIENTS

- Blueberry Jam
- 2 Pie Dough Sheets (Store Bought)

DIRECTIONS

Step 1: In a pie bake-ware, take the 1st pie sheet and cover the inside of the bake-ware. (See Image 1)

Step 2: Now add the blueberry jam inside the pie cavity.

Step 3: Remember not to overflow the filling to the top.

Step 4: Get another pie sheet and cover the top part of your blueberry pie.

Step 5: Trim the excess pie sheet off the bake-ware. Use a fork to seal all the edges of your pie.

Step 6: Air fry at 350°F for 30 minutes or until the pie looks golden brown and crispy on the outside.

Step 7: Allow it to completely cool down before serving.

Note: You can also make the same recipe using puff pastry sheets.

Blueberry Puffs

Prep 5 Min	Cook 5 Min	Four Servings

INGREDIENTS

- Puff Pastry Sheets
- Blueberry Jam

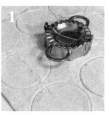

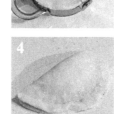
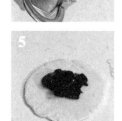
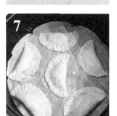

DIRECTIONS

Step 1: Place the pastry sheets dust with a little bit of flour, use a gadget tool called "Dumpling Maker" for easy cut and fold.

Step 2: Put at least 1 tablespoon of blueberry jam then fold to seal. (See Images 2 and 3)

Step 3: Seal the edges by pressing with fork.

Step 4: Air fry at 375°F for 5 minutes Or until golden brown and crispy.

Step 5: Sprinkle castor sugar and Serve.

Note: Two different techniques are shown here, with and without the dumpling maker

Chocolate Chip Cookie

Prep 5 Min	Cook 12 Min	Six Servings

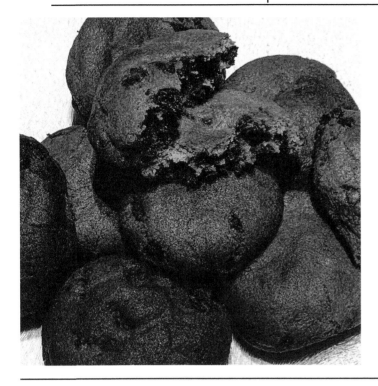

INGREDIENTS

- Chocolate Chip Dough (Store Bought)
- Nutella

DIRECTIONS

Step 1: Take 1 tablespoon full of nutella and place it on the plain plastic surface and let it cool in the refrigerator for 10 minutes.

Step 2: Now take cookie dough and divide into equal portion. (I have taken 2 tablespoons each.)

Step 3: Flatten the cookie dough and place the frozen nutella droplets in the center and fold it like a ball. (See Images 3 and 4)

Step 4: Air fry at 350°F for 12 minutes.

Step 5: Take them out and let it cool down completely before serving.

Note: You can place the cookies on an aluminum foil or you can just air fry the cookies directly as well.

Chocolate Lava Cake

Prep 5 Min	Cook 8 Min	Six Servings

INGREDIENTS

- ½ Cup All-Purpose Flour
- ½ Cup Granulated Sugar
- ¼ Cup Cocoa Powder
- ¼ Cup Vegetable Oil
- ¼ Cup Milk
- 1 Teaspoon Baking Powder
- 6-8 Lindt Lindor

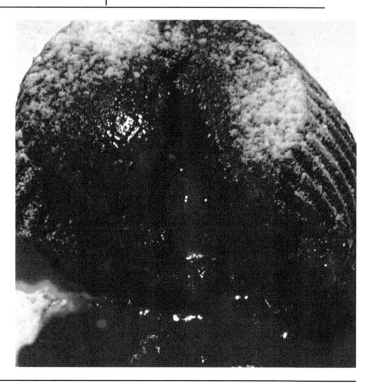

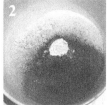

DIRECTIONS

Step 1: In a bowl, combine all the dry ingredients together.

Step 2: Add in the oil and milk. Make a smooth batter.

Step 3: In a silicone baking cup, pour 2 tablespoons of the batter.

Step 4: Place one Lindt Lindor in the middle and then cover it with 2 tablespoons of the batter. (See Image 6)

Step 5: Air fry at 350°F for 8 minutes.

Step 6: Sprinkle castor sugar and serve warm.

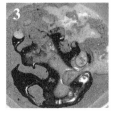
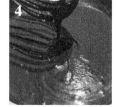

Chocolate Pound Cake

Prep 10 Min	Cook 40 Min	Six Servings

INGREDIENTS

- 1 Cup Milk
- 2 Cups Chocolate Cake Premix
- ¼ Cup Vegetable Oil
- 2 Large Eggs
- ½ Cup Chocolate Chips

DIRECTIONS

Step 1: In a large mixing bowl, take the cake premix, oil, milk, and eggs. Mix until everything is combined very well. But do not over mix it. Then add the chocolate chips and mix again.

Step 2: Spray your loaf pan with cooking spray, and pour the batter into the pan, filling 2/3 the way full.

Step 3: Air fry at 350°F for 15 minutes.

Step 4: Take it out and cover the top with an aluminum foil paper (it prevents the cake top from burning) and air fry again at 350°F for 25 minutes.

Step 5: When the time is up, insert a toothpick and check to see that the toothpick comes out clean. If not, add another 5 minutes.

Note: Allow the cake to completely cool down before slicing it into pieces.

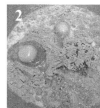

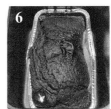

Cinnamon Apple Puff

Prep 5 Min	Cook 10 Min	Six Servings

INGREDIENTS

- 2 Apples
- ¼ Cup Granulated Sugar
- 1 Tablespoon Cinnamon Powder
- Pastry Sheets

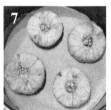

DIRECTIONS

Step 1: Peel the apples and cut it into 3 inches thick rounds. Cut the insides of the apple using baking 1M tip.

Step 2: Mix the cinnamon powder and granulated sugar to make cinnamon sugar.

Step 3: Coat the apple slices with cinnamon sugar. (See Image 3)

Step 4: Cut the pastry sheets into thin strips. (See Image 5)

Step 5: Wrap the pastry sheets around the apple pieces. (See Image 6)

Step 6: Air fry at 350°F for 12 minutes.

Note: Place a crumbled piece of foil paper inside the hole while air frying. This will help retain the hole in the middle after baking as well.

Cinnamon Donut (Biscuits)

Prep 5 Min	Cook 10 Min	Four Servings

INGREDIENTS

- 1 Tablespoon Cinnamon Powder
- ½ Cup Sugar
- ¼ Cup Butter
- Store Bought Biscuit Dough

DIRECTIONS

Step 1: In a clean bowl, mix cinnamon powder and sugar.

Step 2: Take a piece of a biscuit dough and cut out the middle portion. (See Image 2)

Step 3: Apply butter on the donut shaped biscuits.

Step 4: Coat them with the cinnamon sugar mixture.

Step 5: Air fry the donuts at 350°F for 8-10 minutes.

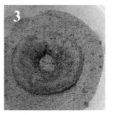

Cinnamon Rolls

Prep 2 Min	Cook 12 Min	Four Servings

INGREDIENTS

- Cinnamon Rolls (Store Bought)

DIRECTIONS

Step 1: Take the store bought cinnamon rolls and place them on to the air fryer basket.

Step 2: Air fry at 350°F for 10 minutes.

Step 3: Flip and cover with aluminum sheet to avoid burning. Air fry again for 5 minutes.

Step 4: Sprinkle the sugar glaze provided with the store bought rolls and serve.

Cream Roll

Prep 10 Min	Cook 12 Min	Four Servings

INGREDIENTS

- Puff Pastry Sheets
- Butter Cream Filling (based on your liking)

DIRECTIONS

Step 1: Cut the pastry sheets into long strips. (See Image 1)

Step 2: Use pastry cones or create a thick oblong form foil for shaping the rolls.

Step 3: Take one strips at a time and wrap it around the pastry cone. (See Image 3)

Step 4: Air fry at 360°F for 9 minutes. Take out and flip and air fry again for 3 minutes.

Step 5: Take out the pastry cone and allow it to cool down completely. Take the cones out slowly by twisting it into circular motion.

Step 6: Fill the insides of the pastry cones with buttercream.

Note: Spray the mould with oil spray to avoid sticking of the pastry dough.

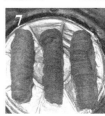

Crème Brulee

Prep 10 Min	Cook 40 Min	Four Servings

INGREDIENTS

- 1 Tablespoon Vanilla Extract
- 3 Large Eggs
- 1 Cup Sugar
- 2 Cups Whipping Cream

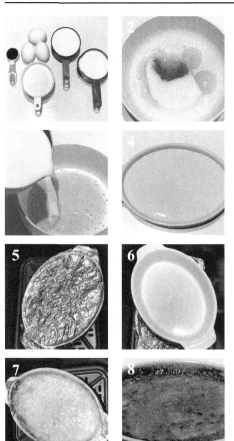

DIRECTIONS

Step 1: In a bowl combine the eggs, sugar, and vanilla extract, mix until smooth.

Step 2: Heat the cream on gas or microwave for 2 minutes (DO NOT BOIL).

Step 3: Take an oven safe baking dish and pour the mixture.

Step 4: Seal it tight with aluminium foil (VERY Important).

Step 5: Air fry at 300°F for 40 minutes.

Step 6: Take it out from the air fryer and let it cool down.

Step 7: Sprinkle sugar on top and air fry at 400°F for 5 minutes (until top layer of sugar is melted/caramelized).

Step 8: Chill it in refrigerator overnight before serving.

Gulab Jamun

Prep 10 Min	Cook 20 Min	Four Servings

INGREDIENTS

For dough

- 2 Cups Gulab Jamun Premix
- ¼ Cup Water
- 4 Tablespoons Ghee

For Sugar Syrup

- 3 Cups Sugar
- 3 Cups Water

DIRECTIONS

Sugar Syrup

Step 1: Put 3 cups of water in a pan on medium flame.

Step 2: To that, add 3 cups of sugar.

Step 3: Boil the sugar mixture for 7-8 minutes or until it becomes little thick in consistency (take a drop and let it cool down for few seconds and touch with your finger, it should feel sticky to touch).

Gulab Jamun

Step 1: For making the dough, add water to the gulab jamun premix and knead it to make a soft dough.

Step 2: Rest for at least 15 minutes.

Step 3: After that knead again and shape them into balls of equal sizes.

Step 4: Apply ghee on your palm and press the balls in between your palm and knead until the balls have no crack on the surface. (See Image 7)

To Be Continued ...

Step 5: Place the balls on an air fryer basket so that there are 2 inches of space in between each ball.

Step 6: Apply ghee generously over the gulab jamun balls.

Step 7: Air fry at 350°F for 16 minutes. Flip each ball every 4 minutes.

Step 8: Put the air-fried jamuns in hot syrup and leave overnight for best result.

Note: Do not place the balls in cold syrup. Let it soak for at least 4-5 hours. Air-fried jamuns take longer to soak than oil fried ones.

Decorate with edible silver foil and rose petals (aka Gulab in Hindi). The rose petals give a nice Gulab flavour.

Mini Chocolate Tart

Prep 5 Min	Cook 10 Min	Eight Servings

INGREDIENTS

- Mini Tart Shells (Store Bought)
- 1 Cup Milk Chocolate Chips
- ½ Cup Whipping Cream
- Kosher Salt Flakes (Optional)

DIRECTIONS

Step 1: Air fry the tart shells at 350°F for 8-10 minutes (until golden brown).

Step 2: Heat the whipping cream (DO NOT BOIL) and pour onto the chocolate chips. Let it sit for 2-3 minutes.

Step 3: Mix the chocolate and cream together.

Step 4: Pour the mixture into the air-fried tart shells and refrigerate until the chocolate creams thickens up.

Note: Sprinkle some kosher salt on top and serve shilled!

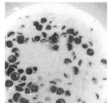

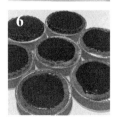

Mini Mixed-Berry Tart

Prep 5 Min	Cook 18 Min	Ten Servings

INGREDIENTS

- 2 Cups Mixed Berries (Frozen)
- ¼ Cup Corn Starch
- ¼ Cup Sugar
- Mini Tart Shells (Store Bought)

DIRECTIONS

Step 1: In a bowl, mix the frozen mixed-berries with corn starch and sugar.

Step 2: Pour the berry mixture into the tart shells. (See Image 5)

Step 3: Place the tart shells in a preheated airfryer. Air fry at 330°F for 15-18 minutes.

Step 4: Take out and allow to cool before serving.

Note: Use monk-fruit sweetener instead of sugar if you want to avoid sugar. I use monk-fruit sweetener on a regular basis for this one.

Nutella Twist

Prep 10 Min	Cook 10 Min	Ten Servings

INGREDIENTS

- Puff Pastry Sheets
- Nutella Spread

DIRECTIONS

Step 1: Place the pastry sheets, and start to spread the Nutella chocolate spread onto the whole area of the pastry sheets.

Step 2: Roll them on both sides to achieve just like in the given image. (See Images 3 and 4)

Step 3: Now cut them up into 2 inches thickness just like in the image.

Step 4: Place them in an air fryer basket in one layer keeping distance in-between because they will puff up and expand.

Step 5: Air fry at 350°F for 8 minutes, flip and cook on other side for 4 minutes.

Note: Sprinkle powdered sugar on top.

Nutella-Stuffed Croissant

Prep 5 Min	Cook 15 Min	Two Servings

INGREDIENTS

- Croissant Dough/Sheets (Store Bought)
- Nutella Spread
- Walnuts (Crushed)

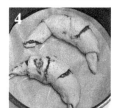
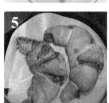

DIRECTIONS

Step 1: First, you need to unroll the dough sheet and cut out the triangles for easy rolling.

Step 2: Generously spread nutella. (See Image 1)

Step 3: Add generous amount of crushed walnuts onto the croissant.

Step 4: Roll the croissants as shown in the image (starting from the wide side first).

Step 5: Air fry at 360°F for 12 minutes. Flip and air fry again for 2-3 minutes.

Note: Sprinkle powdered sugar and serve!

Oreo Cheesecake

Prep 10 Min	Cook 40 Min	Four Servings

INGREDIENTS

- 1 Tablespoon Melted Butter
- 8-10 Pieces Oreo Cookie
- ¼ Cup Condensed Milk
- 1 Large Egg
- 1 Brick Cream Cheese
- 1 Tablespoon Vanilla Extract
- ¼ Cup Whipping Cream

DIRECTIONS

Step 1: In a food processor, crush the Oreo cookies and pour in the melted butter and combine them together very well.

Step 2: To make the filling take the cream cheese, vanilla extract, egg, and the condensed milk in a large bowl. Mix and make sure to have a nice and smooth consistency.

Step 3: Now add the whipping cream and mix thoroughly once again. (See Image 5)

Step 4: Line the springform pan with parchment paper.

Step 5: Pour in the Oreo-butter mixture and press with the back of your finger/spoon. (See Image 7)

Step 6: Fill in the cream-cheese filling and seal it with aluminium foil.

Step 7: Air fry at 315°F for 40 minutes.

Step 8: Remove from air fryer and refrigerate for a minimum of 2 hours.

Step 9: Serve with a topping of your choice or just chocolate syrup for a better taste.

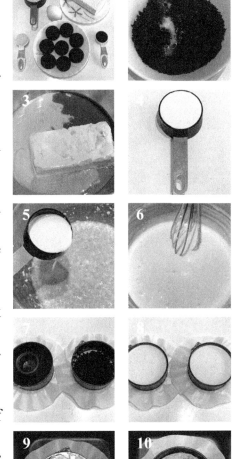

Raspberry Jam Biscuit

Prep 5 Min	Cook 15 Min	Four Servings

INGREDIENTS

- Biscuit Dough (Store Bought)
- Raspberry Jam
- 2 Tablespoons Butter

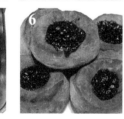

DIRECTIONS

Step 1: Take one slice of the biscuit dough and make a cavity/ dent in the middle where you can put the raspberry jam.

Step 2: Generously brush butter on the biscuit.

Step 3: Fill the cavity with 1 tablespoon full of raspberry jam.

Step 4: Place at least 4-5 pieces of the jam-filled biscuits into the preheated air fryer.

Step 5: Air fry at 350°F for 9 minutes. Remove the basket, cover the biscuits with an aluminium foil (this will prevent it from burning), air fry again at 350°F for 7 minutes.

Note: You can use any jam of your choice.

Semiya Payasam

Prep 10 Min	Cook 40 Min	Four Servings

INGREDIENTS

- ¼ Cup Semiya
- 1 Cup Khoya
- ½ Cup Condensed Milk
- 1 Cup Full Fat Milk
- 1 Tablespoon Raisins
- 1 Tablespoon Crushed Cashews
- ½ Tablespoon Ghee
- Crushed Cardamom (2-3)

DIRECTIONS

Step 1: In a microwave safe bowl, add milk, khoya, condensed milk, and crushed cardamom. Give it a good mix.

Step 2: Microwave the mixture for 5 minutes. Your rabdi mix is ready.

Step 3: Heat ghee in a pan and put the semiya. Roast the semiya until it turns brown. (See Image 5)

Step 4: In an 8 inch cake pan pour the rabdi mixture, add roasted semiya along with raisins and cashews. Mix everything.

Step 5: Seal the cake pan with aluminium foil. Air fryer at 330°F for 40 minutes.

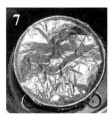

Sugar Puff (Super Easy Dessert)

Prep 5 Min	Cook 8 Min	Four Servings

INGREDIENTS

- Pastry Sheets
- 1 Tablespoon of Brown Sugar

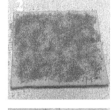

DIRECTIONS

Step 1: Unwrap the puff pastry sheets. Cut the pastry sheets into 6 inch squares.

Step 2: Cut the pastry sheets into 2 inches thick strips. (See Image 1)

Step 3: Sprinkle brown sugar on to the pastry sheet.

Step 4: Roll the pastry sheet from bottom up.

Step 5: Place the sugar puffs in an air fryer basket and air fry at 360°F for 6-8 minutes.

Cooking Conversion Chart

WEIGHT

IMPERIAL	METRIC
1/2 oz	15 g
1 oz	29 g
2 oz	57 g
3 oz	85 g
4 oz	113 g
5 oz	141 g
6 oz	170 g
8 oz	227 g
10 oz	283 g
12 oz	340 g
13 oz	369 g
14 oz	397 g
15 oz	425 g
1 lb	453 g

TEMPERATURE

FAHRENHEIT	CELSIUS
100 °F	37 °C
150 °F	65 °C
200 °F	93 °C
250 °F	121 °C
300 °F	150 °C
325 °F	160 °C
350 °F	180 °C
375 °F	190 °C
400 °F	200 °C
425 °F	220 °C
450 °F	230 °C
500 °F	260 °C
525 °F	274 °C
550 °F	288 °C

MEASUREMENT

CUP	ONCES	MILLILITERS	TBSP
8 cup	64 oz	1895 ml	128
6 cup	48 oz	1420 ml	96
5 cup	40 oz	1180 ml	80
4 cup	32 oz	960 ml	64
2 cup	16 oz	500 ml	32
1 cup	8 oz	250 ml	16
3/4 cup	6 oz	177 ml	12
2/3 cup	5 oz	158 ml	11
1/2 cup	4 oz	118 ml	8
3/8 cup	3 oz	90 ml	6
1/3 cup	2.5 oz	79 ml	5.5
1/4 cup	2 oz	59 ml	4
1/8 cup	1 oz	30 ml	3
1/16 cup	1/2 oz	15 ml	1

Acknowledgement

This book wouldn't have been possible without the efforts and genius of my freaking amazing designer, **Tahmid**, and my super talented editor/proofreader, **Ankita**. No words can express how thankful I feel to have you both on my side ☺

I would also like to thank GBP author **Joseph Cassis** for trying my recipes and giving me his honest and amazing feedback that lead me to believe that this book's recipes are cook-worthy.

Lastly, I want to thank my **Maa** and **Papa** for being on my side and always encouraging and inspiring me with great cooking skills ... You see I got that "Gene" in me ☺

About Susmita!

Susmita's #1 passion in life had been cooking. During her childhood days, her papa was the person who always encouraged her cooking by eating her initial days of "not so good cooking experiments".

As she grew older, her career took over her passion for cooking but this did stop her from cooking. She now managed to teach herself easy and delicious food which was less complicated and took less preparation time.

And then her entrepreneurial endeavors started (Susmita is the founder and CEO of Global Book Publishing). Sadly, this resulted in even less time for her love for cooking. Cooking is a "Stress-Buster" for her and she could be found cooking (mostly Baking) in the wee hours of the night after she had a stressful workday.

Air-Fryer changed her life for good. She now cooks and bakes absolutely delicious food in no time. Her family enjoys every meal and she enjoys her happy days of cooking YUMMY Food.

Through this book, she wants to share her home-cooked delicious food which can help busy ladies all around the world.

You can join her and share your stories and food too:

Printed in Great Britain
by Amazon

35951807R00071